A FRIDAY NIGHT LIGHTS COMPANION

OTHER SMART POP TELEVISION TITLES

Contents

A FRIDAY NIGHT LIGHTS COMPANION

Introduction

As a rule, I am a composed, stoic person, constitutionally hard-wired to keep my emotions to myself. This is a byproduct of growing up in the Midwest, I suspect. It's not that showing emotion is a sign of weakness among my family in Central Illinois; it's just considered unnecessary, a distraction, *too much fuss.* If you have a problem, you keep it to yourself, and you get over it. This is not always the most healthy way to live one's life. Lord knows I've witnessed enough Thanksgiving blowups to know that eventually, inevitably, the tightly wound coils snap. But it's the way I was raised, and that's the way I'm always going to be. Say what you will, but it works for me.

And particularly: I do not cry. The last time I cried, it was 1982. I was six, I'd fallen off my bike into a pile of gravel, and I sprinted home to my mother. She took me into the bathroom, poured rubbing alcohol on my bleeding knee, wiped my face with a towel, and told me to knock it off. "Crying won't heal your knee faster," she said, smiling but firm. "And crying lets your knee win." I don't remember crying after that, not even at my grandmother's funeral six years ago. I was sad. But I didn't cry. I saw my dad cry once, at his father-in-law's funeral. We followed behind the hearse in silence, and then, suddenly, he burst into a crazed, explosive two-second wail. He then blew his nose, grunted, and said, "My underwear must have been too tight there." He hasn't cried since. I don't think there's anything *wrong* with crying. I just don't do it.

Except. Except.

I do not know why it is—this phenomenon is honestly terrifying to me—but every single time I have ever watched an episode of *Friday Night Lights*, I damned near start weeping. I don't, mind you; I always fight it off. But as much as I would like to, I cannot deny it. Something about that show turns me almost primal; I find myself doing a lot of fist-biting, throat-clearing, and "boy, the pollen count is high today." This is bizarre. I have had truly tragic events occur in my life, and I have not been near tears. But *Friday Night Lights* just destroys me. It doesn't even have to be a sad scene. The music gets going, the camera zooms in, people start talking . . . and man, I'm just done.

This means something, I think.

Perhaps the most amazing thing about *Friday Night Lights* is that it is painfully, breathtakingly realistic and yet also exists as some sort of platonic ideal of what human beings can be like.

The show has often been praised for its unflinching handling of hot-button issues like abortion, racism, and war, but even using the phrase "hot-button" seems like an insult, almost crass, to the show itself, much the same way it might be in life. If someone in your family was contemplating an abortion, you would never think of that decision as a "hot-button" issue; it would be a family issue, dealt with in personal terms, privately. And that's how it feels when Becky goes through the same situation in on *Friday Night*

Lights. It's not something that has anything to do with politics, or religion, or whatever people on both sides of the "debate" try to attach to it. It's a wrenching, intensely personal situation, and a decision made (and experienced) entirely by the people involved, not those from the outside. *Friday Night Lights* made me feel like I was on the inside. *Friday Night Lights* made me feel like I was part of the family. *Friday Night Lights* made me feel like I was more a part of real life than actually being a part of real life.

This is what great art—and this is what we're talking about here, art—can do: It can transport us, make us a part of something that we never could have been otherwise. A large part of the genius of *Friday Night Lights* is, of course, that it never seems like art; it would never be nearly as powerful and moving if it did. (It is far more interested in telling a story than trying to impress critics . . . which is probably why they were so impressed, actually.) No, it feels like life. I don't mean life the way that I live it, or you live it, or even as it actually exists. It is, after all, just a television show. But it *feels* like life, the way we would like to imagine life is, not a fantasy land filled with fairies and ninjas and happy endings, but instead full of huge-hearted, achingly human characters wrestling with tragedy, with fear, with pain . . . and ultimately winning. There is a hope inside every single character on *Friday Night Lights* that I can only wish every human in real life has, that I dream is still a part of even the most hardened, beaten-down individual. Everyone on *Friday Night Lights* is trying. They all still believe.

I don't always see that in life. But I see that in *Friday Night Lights.* I see hope.

There's a temptation, like with any item of entertainment that is shared and beloved by a small and passionate number of people, for me to just start talking to you about my favorite moments in the show. After all, I know you're someone who loves it as much as I do. I look forward to, in the coming years, when more and more people discover the show on DVD, when they come to that realization that, *Holy cow, this show is amazing. Why wasn't I watching this?* I'm so envious of them. They still get to experience it for the first time.

You, you've picked up this book, so you already know. You know about Smash, and Lyla, and Landry and Tyra (even if you're still trying to forget that first episode of season two), and Jason, and the new kids Luke and Vince and Jess and Becky and even Hastings, and the Riggins brothers, and Tim's sacrifice. If I am not careful, I will list them all. They feel like old friends. The rest of this book does a better job of talking about all of them, and what they meant to various writers, than I would. I feel like I'm too close to them.

With all the kids around, it's worth remembering the anchors of the show, "Coach and Mrs. Coach," a walking refutation to the maxim that a television couple is only interesting if they're not together. I am not the least bit ashamed to admit that, as a newly married man, I have studiously watched Eric and Tami and used them as a model for my upcoming years of marriage. I've learned to be patient, to be reasonable, to be understanding, to share, to compromise and, in a pinch, to just be quiet and *listen*. Every marriage I ever see on television, in movies, anywhere in popular media, is always unhappy or fraught with betrayal, or so cartoonish as to keep reminding me that it's fictional. Not here. I want the Taylors to be my parents, and I want to be them as parents. It might even be cool to carry around a whistle.

Everyone has a favorite character, though, and mine, perhaps not surprisingly, is Matt, a kinda nerdy, almost average kid when we first meet him who ends up being sort of Dillon's version of Job. Yet, through it all, he remains strong, and willful, and, yes, hopeful. He's gonna need that strength and will and hope, too, if he's gonna be Coach's son-in-law.

But there I go again, talking about everyone like they're my friends, like they exist, like we've all known each other for years. That's what *Friday Night Lights* inspires: the sense that it is real life, only heightened, with a logical narrative. And that's what brings out emotions that are dulled by the daily runaround, and lets them feel true, feel pure, feel raw. This is the way I want the world to be. This is the way the world should be.

Again, though: You know all this. So just dig in to this book, relive all your favorite moments, visit with old friends. This book, in a way, is sort of like a yearbook; part of me wants to have everyone from Dillon sign it for me, to remember all the good times, to *see them next year, have a great summer!* I feel like I can pop on over and have them do it, too. I really do.

Plus, reading about *Friday Night Lights* is *far* less likely to make me cry than watching *Friday Night Lights*. Which I do even still, when I've seen every episode so many times. But don't tell anyone. Least of all my dad. I'll just claim my underwear's too tight.

Will Leitch
June 2011

Texas Forever

Friday Night Lights and the Quest for Authenticity

ADAM WILSON

1. But What Does Matt Saracen Dream About?

I'm a Reagan baby, a product of recession, later reared in the eco-
nomically secure Clinton nineties, in a McMansioned suburb of
the Eastern Seaboard. In nearby Boston, the athletes of interest
preside in professional Parks and Gardens. They are televised,
billboarded, extra-life-sized for us aesthetes to admire as we turn,
finally, from our dissertations, to catch the last inning or quarter,
becoming vicarious Americans, populist fist-pumpers in the soft
reflection of our plasma flat screens.

My own sports career ended at fifteen, soon after my discov-
eries of breasts and marijuana—plus, my postpubic body's physiological rejection of the command, "Run laps." I attended a large
public high school known for its high rate of alumni acceptance
into Harvard and for its unattractive cheerleaders. Once at a bas-
ketball game, a rival school's fans chanted, "Who Let the Dogs
Out" when our Lady-Lions took the court.

The school was demographically diverse: half Jewish, one-quarter genius-Asian, 5 percent bussed-in black kids, and a small minority of miscellaneous Christians—"We killed Christ" was a popular cafeteria taunt aimed at the one Gentile among my friends. Dillon, Texas, this was not. Our football coach smartly nixed the ambitious passing game in favor of an all-run offense that was "less embarrassing." We had no sandy-haired, steel-eyed Tim Riggins to root for. No tragic Smash Williams, whose shattered knee meant shattered dreams. Not even a heroic survivor like Jason Street to prod spirit into our allegiance-less hearts. We'd never heard of a rally girl, and had certainly never imagined she might bear any resemblance to lovely Lyla or tawdry Tyra.[1]

Still, one makes do. When it comes to social strata in American public schools, life has no choice but to imitate, if not art, then at least John Hughes movies. Our football players held top position in the high school hierarchy. They wore jerseys over ties on game day, took creatine, shotgunned beers, spoke with put-on Boston accents, had bonfires at "The Point," rode dad-bought Jeep Wranglers down our mean suburban streets. They even whacked freshmen with wooden paddles a la *Dazed and Confused*.

Sensitive stoners like me hung girl-less at the edge of the party, colluding in the mass self-delusion that *this* was a football team, that *this* was a party. We watched with envy as our outsized peers spat cheap game to the glitter-lipped girls. It was not what I had in mind.

College was better, but marginally. I attended a second-tier private university where half the students rode the predental track in a race of immeasurably boring, if well-groomed, horses. If nothing else, they had nice smiles. At least some percentage participated in

---

1 In fairness to my female classmates, I must make the concession that *no* high school students *anywhere* look like Minka Kelly and Adrianne Palicki, who even in season one were at least five years above high school age.

the *Animal House*-inspired performance art piece entitled, "Drink until you're blind; make out with anything that moves."

Our football team was named after a circus elephant. We battled other comically mascotted schools: Camels, White Mules, Polar Bears, Ephs, and, intriguingly, Lord Jeff's. Attendance was higher at girls' soccer. Still, there was a football frat. They did football frat things, like punch and vomit, haze and sexually harass. Our quarterback even courted our class' token celebrity, an actress acknowledged less for her acting abilities than for her impressively muscled butt cheeks.

I once saw the two of them, arms linked, slow-strolling frat row like demented royalty, crowned by crooked baseball caps, surrounded by an entourage of adoring, cargo-pantsed yes-men. Looking back I think: how deeply ingrained our American myths; even the most privileged among us feel inclined to act them out.

I, too, acted out fantasies, though not the sexual ones I'd imagined with my previously mentioned classmate. But my sports career was resuscitated on the school's greeneries, where I discovered the joyous exercise in inebriated hand-eye coordination commonly known as keg-softball. I captained a team of fringe weirdos and druggies called The Flying Heads. Our ragtag band of misfits was meant to beat the evil football frat in a miraculous come-from-behind victory a la every sports film from *Bad News Bears* on. Unfortunately, half the Heads ingested psychedelic mushrooms before the game. We saw balls where there was only sky. It was a landslide loss.

Still, we beat on, bats against the current. I hit my first "over-the-fence" home run in May 2004, just prior to graduation, a feat that's slow-trot muscle memory carried me lazily through two years of post collegiate unemployment.

I spent the first year lonely in Austin, Texas, searching for versions of the Middle South I'd seen in films from Spaghetti Westerns to Richard Linklater's *Slacker*. This world was not to be found.

No sweet-drawling diner waitress ever whispered my name. No hipster-barista offered to buy me a coffee while I deconstructed Faulkner. No señorita sauteed pork loin in my kitchenette wearing only a T-shirt, hips and hair swaying to the sound of some distant, inaudible salsa.

I did, however, briefly hold a job that involved standing for eight straight hours at a highway exit ramp holding a giant orange arrow. I did learn what a "prison burrito" is (Doritos mixed with dry ramen noodles). I did live in a neighborhood where parts of *Friday Night Lights* would later be shot.

Eventually my car got stolen. I ran out of money.

Knowing no other narrative to fall back on, I moved to New York City to become a writer. Endured "hardships" commonly proliferated by indie films: bookstore employment, whiskey-posing, cockroaches, squandered romance. Spent Saturdays honing stories of small tragedy, overwrought, filled with *Seinfeld*-aping observational humor and fantastical oral sex.

I watched *Friday Night Lights* for the first time in my studio apartment, bedridden by the idiocy of avoiding a flu shot. Some cable channel had the first season on marathon so sick boys like myself could feel the pull of pigskin, forget our ailing, gene-weak bodies amidst the rush of Panther pride and the knowledge that no woman in a million years will ever out-MILF Ms. Tami Taylor.

Which is all to say: When I lie in bed at night and imagine white-bearded God making his earthly presence known at the foot of my futon, he asks, "And what is your deepest desire, young man?" I say, "Lord of all things, king of the universe, pur-veyor of rain, and pain, and occasional love, would you be so kind as to turn me into Tim Riggins?"

Suddenly, I have morphed into the Panther fullback himself: majestic in blue and gold, #33, cheekbones the product of seri-ously intelligent design, sweat-wet locks hanging freely from my helmet; clear eyes, full heart, and Tyra, Lyla, and all the other Dillon

Debbies, and debutantes, and dirty, flirty rally girls, watching with want as I strut to the huddle, back-pat Matt Saracen, move my beautiful body to the line of scrimmage, Texas forever.

2. Real Americans

My generation is obsessed with authenticity. We backpack to the far reaches of civilization in search of land untarnished by tourism. Read nonfiction with scrupulous eyes, wary of deception from the next James Frey. Use San Marzano tomatoes in our sauce. Lionize bands only after the singer has committed suicide. Spend big bucks on high-end vintage clothing, then scoff at those wearing cheaper, faux-vintage duds. Speculate on the scriptedness of reality shows. Correct our parents' pronunciation of foreign words—"The 'J' is silent, Dad!"

A psychoanalyst might posit that we are a generation overcompensating for what we perceive to be our own lack of authenticity. That global-techno-culture and late capitalism have irreversibly blurred the lines between reality and virtual reality, between art and commerce, between love and the syrupy, shallow version of it perpetuated by Hollywood and Hallmark. That, amidst this barrage of force-fed narratives, we must grasp, in futility, for any terra firma. The layman might say we are a generation of pretentious assholes.

These analyses hold especially true of people with my shared background: white, educated, upper middle class, and burdened by the guilt of all three. To wit:

One house on my block was smaller than the others. It had cheap siding and was surrounded on all sides by a chain-link fence. A barking dog was chained to the fence. A rusty car was up on blocks in the driveway. Shirtless blond boys hovered. My family called these people "The Real Americans."

The implication being that everyone else we knew—ourselves included—were "Fake Americans." Our high school had a "fake" football team, "fake" cheerleaders. Even our most attractive girls were surgically enhanced in the breasts and noses, literally fake. My friends and I would talk about Real America like it was some distant land, war-torn but beautiful. A place where sadness was earned, and everyone got laid.

I fetishized our Real American neighbors, watched them with equal parts envy and earnest curiosity. They weren't particularly interesting to watch. They rode bikes and watched TV and had barbeques in the summer. They didn't seem any happier or sadder or drunker or sexier or smarter or handsomer or uglier than anyone else I knew. They weren't special. I came to the difficult but paradoxically self-elevating conclusion that these "Real" Real Americans weren't like the "Fake" Real Americans in movies. Unlike, say, tenderhearted Steel Town running back Tom Cruise in *All the Right Moves*, a poet's soul wasn't buried deep beneath the veneer of philistinism. The realization was difficult because it meant the death of certain romantic notions. It was also self-elevating because it meant I wasn't missing out on anything. Or was I?

When I moved to Austin it was in search of this Real America, in search of a way either to realize or definitively destroy my Real American fantasy. When H.G. Bissinger wrote the book *Friday Night Lights*, his exposé of high-school-football-obsessed Odessa, Texas, he, too, was in search of authenticity, in search of uneasy truths overlooked by Hollywood. The book's harsh light stripped the shiny gloss from Texas high school football, displaying the traumas and exploitations that scaffold this celebrated pastime.

But for readers of my background, the book held another, inadvertent effect. It worked to alleviate the perpetually itchy idea that life would be better had we been born with golden throwing arms in place of our silver spoons.

Bissinger's book told us we were wrong. That being QB1 wasn't all it was cracked up to be. It told of injuries, Jesus indoctrination, horrible racism, insurmountable pressure. What's more, Bissinger revealed that glory itself is short-lived. At eighteen you're burnt. Life ends. The beautiful cheerleader has become a pregnant beast. Your scholarship has been revoked. Your career prospects are unpromising. You'll never leave Odessa.

Unintentionally, *Friday Night Lights* the book presented a vision of rural life in America that confirmed the worst fears of the urban bourgeoisie, thus further solidifying the status quo. And though the book contains its share of highly sympathetic characters—well drawn, brimming with humanity—the overall impression is of Texas as an alien land, curiously foreign, its hats and spurs as exotic as an African tribesman's drooping ears.

When Peter Berg made *Friday Night Lights* into a film, there was concern from both the book's fans and arbiters of highbrow authenticity that the studio would strip Bissinger's book of the grittiness that made it great, made it real. That Hollywood would turn Bissinger's downer of a book into some bullshit-romantic treatise on the resilience of the human spirit. Glory would be glorified; they'd airbrush out the sadness to aid in mass digestion.

This concern wasn't completely justified; the film includes a hair-raising scene of domestic violence and ends on a less-than-hopeful losing note. Still, the transformation from book to film, from nonfiction to fiction, from cultural investigation to commercial commodity, reeked of artistic and journalistic compromise.

When NBC decided to adapt *Friday Night Lights* for TV, these same purists (read: snobs) pounded fists against the wall. TV, the story goes, does not deal in art or journalism. It does not deal in complexity or subtlety. It manipulates, tricks. It is untrustworthy. It is cheap, trashy, exploitative. It is glaringly unrealistic.

This broad-spectrum criticism of the medium itself is pompous and ignorant, of course, but it also points to a growing and problematic tendency among contemporary highbrow culture critics, a tendency to confuse high-budget fidelity with artfulness, verisimilitude with authenticity, "grittiness" with emotional truth. Only when something "feels real" is it deemed worthy of inclusion into the contemporary canon.

Friday Night Lights occupies an odd place in a TV world that likes its commodities easily categorized. Hour-long dramas (comedies demand a separate discussion) on HBO, Showtime, and AMC have high production values, limited commercial interruptions, swearing, and in many cases, nudity. It is for these shallow signifiers of high art that shows on these channels are branded "Good TV," regardless of actual qualitative measures like writing and acting. Think of *The Wire*, perhaps the hippest and most beloved series of the current era, whose Bissinger-esque unsparing grotesquerie and attention to issues like race, education, and politics appear to have blinded the show's fans (I am among them) to its hit-or-wildly-miss acting and its glaringly ridiculous plot elements (e.g., all of season five).

Networks like NBC, with their commercial interruptions, lack of swearing and nudity, and populist pandering to broader audiences, produce what is commonly referred to as "Trash," or "Bad TV." The finest of these specimens—addictive melodramas like *Lost*—find themselves whacked with backhanded tags like "guilty pleasure."

Friday Night Lights' lo-fi, hi-def handi-cam look, nonfictional roots, and willingness to engage seriously in heavy thematic material—the Iraq War, race, class, etc.—suggest the show might easily cross over into the "Good TV" pantheon. But *Friday Night Lights*' emphatic un-realisticness—its embrace of cliché and its disinterest in sticking to the facts provided by its paperback predecessor—makes this a difficult argument to make against detractors who think all TV that doesn't adhere to the HBO/Showtime/AMC formula is trash.

3. What We Talk About When We Talk About Tim Riggins

What I'm getting at is that to try to read the show *Friday Night Lights* as a work of realism—a twice-watered-down reproduction of a journalistic text—is both to misread it and to be disappointed by it.

This is not to say that the show doesn't contain realistic elements or make use of realist techniques. On the contrary, *Friday Night Lights'* handheld camera style makes the show feel like a documentary. Same goes for the casting of actors such as Jessie Plemons (Landry Clarke), whose acne-scarred face marks him as distinctly unplastic, distinctly "real." But by giving the show this docu-realist feel, *Friday Night Lights'* creators have inadvertently armed skeptic viewers with an expectation of realistic-ness, an expectation that the show will stick closely to its nonfiction roots.

This expectation most certainly cannot be fulfilled by a show whose cast includes actresses like Minka Kelly, who is clearly ten years older in real life than her character, Lyla, a high school student; a show in which the plotlines include a mysteriously never-spoken-of-again murder committed by one of its main characters, and the exponentially improbable courtship by that same character of a woman so far out of his league she's doing end zone dances at the Super Bowl while he's stuck in Pop Warner; a show whose reliable husband ultimately apologizes to his wife *every* single time he's done something wrong, and even sometimes when he hasn't; a show whose romantic lead belongs to a level of handsomeness so far above that of the average human male that it's unclear whether he was birthed from a human womb or sprung immaculately from the head of some teen-girl-Zeus' sexual fantasy.

All of which begs the question: if we can't assess the quality of this show based on its approximation of real life, how then can we assess it? If it isn't an attempt at realism, what is it?

To my eye, *Friday Night Lights* draws from a number of traditions that date back as far Greek myths, the New Testament, the fairy tale, and the literary epic. Tim Riggins is a Christlike figure with his long hair and the way he suffers for the sins of others (namely his brother, Billy). Surely it is no accident that he wears number thirty-three. Like Don Quixote, Riggins rides the open plains—he's traded his horse for a pickup—saving damsels in distress. Like Odysseus, he has reigned victorious on the battlefield but must fight off sirens on his long trek home. Like Luke Skywalker, he is an orphan who learns the art of living from a proverb-spouting master. Like Cinderella, he was raised by trollish and insufferable relatives. Like Don Juan, he spreads female thighs with but a wink of his sea-blue eyes. Like Poseidon, Riggins literally controls the tides. Consider: West Texas is barren, dry. Tumbleweeds pass like old lovers, whispering harsh hellos. Rain gods are prayed to; prayers are denied. Yet how many times have we seen Riggins standing in a storm, soaking wet for our sins, awaiting the rejuvenating kiss of some fair maiden?

And like Sir Galahad, Riggins is on a quest for a holy grail.

As *Friday Night Lights* is a modern show in a postmodern world, Riggins' quest is not for some tangible object—a trophy, say, though he wants that, too—but for an elusive intangible. But like my younger, soul-searching self, and like my generational compatriots in search of authenticity, the tragedy of Tim Riggins is his futile quest for an immaterial concept, for our old friend Real America; he is searching for something called "Texas Forever."

4. Pulling Out of Here to Win

In almost every movie about athletes in a small town, the protagonist's goal is to escape from it. In *All the Right Moves*, Tom Cruise needs a football scholarship so he can avoid a lifetime in

the steel mill. In *Varsity Blues*, James Van Der Beek needs a football scholarship so he can major in Women's Studies at Brown.
And not just athletes; in *8 Mile* Eminem must hone his rap skills in
order to escape the fate of his trailer park; in *Good Will Hunting*,
Matt Damon must get a corporate job so he can stop wasting his
genius doing construction.

The towns presented in these films are blue collar, and the implication seems to be that working-class life has its quiet charms but
is ultimately unsatisfactory for anyone with "talent." And though
this hackneyed narrative might, on the surface, seem inspirational
for the small-town boy who wants to be the first in his family to
go to college, or the barrio princess who dreams of being a NASA
scientist, it also quietly affirms the status quo; it condescends by
painting red-state America as "one-horse" and outdated, a place
unsuitable for the chosen few who, like Jacob, were simply born
with dubious birthrights.

Television shows are less drawn to the "getting out" narrative,
for the simple reason that "getting out" is antithetical to a show's
goal of continuing week after week, season after season. The cli-
chéd ending, in which we view our hero escaping, Springsteen-
style, in a rusty Ford, winding down the highway into the promise
of American opportunity, is only possible in the very final episode
of a show. Most TV show creators want their shows to be picked
up by the network, year after year, and are, by nature, more interested in creating a plurality of open-ended scenarios. In this, TV
is possibly the only art form that mirrors real life—at least in the
midst of a show's run—by allowing narratives to pile up on one
another, allowing conflicts to remain extendedly unresolved.

Think of Matt Saracen. His arc at first appears to fit the traditional "getting out" model. But by nature of the show's continuity we are able to confront the consequences of "getting
out." We are able to see that escape itself is no solution, but
only the door to different problems. We see that assimilation into

the urban, educated world is not always desirable. This is why Saracen returns from Chicago—at least for a while—to Grandma, and Julie, and the harsh beauty of the Texas plains that offer their own, multifaceted appeal.

Saracen, of course, is not the show's only character. It is to *Friday Night Lights'* great credit, though, that among the show's many characters, we are privy to a wide array of dreams and realities, not all of them trite or obvious. Within the show's many households we see nuanced delineations of class and strata rarely examined on American television (*The Wire*, perhaps, being the strongest exception). Not only that, but we are presented with a variety of family structures—one parent, two parents, no parent, parent in Iraq leaving kid with senile grandma, etc.—that do well to represent contemporary America's movement beyond the nuclear family.

Consider the socioeconomic diversity of these characters in relation to their counterparts on *Gossip Girl*, where one is either an heiress or "from Williamsburg." Or on *The O.C.*, where only by infiltrating the bourgeoisie can Ryan create a "good life" for himself.

These shows view class as distinctly black or white, rich or poor, employer or employee, mud-covered or glamorous. "Poor" characters are signified by ragged clothing, disintegrating homes, and a disposition to alcoholism. "Rich" characters are signified by the accessories of high fashion, luxurious mansions, and also, oddly, by a disposition to alcoholism. Rarely do we see a lower-middle-class family, like the Taylors, satisfied with its cultural lot, dressed normally, and moderate in its use of alcohol. At its best *Friday Night Lights* portrays the complexity of contemporary American life with true candor, sans concession to ratings-raising melodrama.

Take the way *Friday Night Lights* dealt with Matt Saracen's Iraq-stationed father. There was no "special Iraq episode," complete with teary good-byes and underlying political commentary about the importance of supporting our troops. Neither was there equal and opposite left-wing indoctrination, with the show making its point about the idiocy of Bush and the evil father who has abandoned his son so he can kill innocents overseas.

Rather, Saracen's father is a complex figure, morally gray. He is a character who has made difficult choices and continues to do so. A character who is allowed the nobility of self-contradiction.

Likewise, Tim Riggins may be a demigod, but the stark contrast between Riggins' blessed bone structure and the pocked cheeks of Landry Clarke alone illuminates Landry's humanity, positions him as relatable, "real." If Riggins is our über-mensch, then Landry is the everyman: smart but not a genius, ugly but not hideous, sad but not suicidal. Like Riggins, he transcends the boundaries of class and location to become a universally recognizable archetype without sacrificing the warts and idiosyncrasies that prevent him from becoming a cliché.

5. Texas Forever

But back to Riggins. Tim Riggins has no particular interest in "getting out." He accompanied Jason Street to New York and it wasn't for him. He tried college at San Antonio State and dropped out before he'd even arrived on campus. He's attempted a number of professions that might have eased his slide into the white-collar world. Alas, he's better off in cowboy boots.

What Riggins wants, in fact, is something far more complex than money or status, wine or women. What he wants is so complex, so poetically vague and out of reach, that he can't even explain what it is in any way other than to stare at a sunset and say, "Texas Forever" in a way that makes us understand he both paradoxically already has what he wants—a Texas sunset, wind in his hair—and never will, because what he wants is only a feeling, and it's fleeting.

Which is not to say that Tim Riggins doesn't also long for certain discrete solutions. He would like a supportive family, a loving lady, and enough money to keep him out of trouble, comfortable in the business of fixing cars and drinking beer. But as in any great Western, these material wants pale in comparison to Riggins' true desire, which is the mystical and metaphorical place called Texas Forever, a place whose appeal lies partly in the unspoken profundity of its landscape—the wide roads and wider skies—and partly in the notions of liberty and freedom upon which, as the saying goes, this country was founded.

6. Dreams from My Father

Here's my family's origin myth: My father flew into New York from London in 1976, on the day before the celebration of the Bicentennial. Twin Towers loomed like silver stalks amidst a pink horizon. First meal was at Tom's Restaurant, which was not yet the Seinfeld Restaurant. The waitress called him "honey." He thought, "America."

He stayed on. Saw Springsteen sing "Rosalita" to a half-empty crowd at the Palladium. Saw Chris Chambliss lift one into the left-field bleachers. When he returned to England he carried this romantic America the way one carries a beloved paperback whose actual text has been buried by the inference of the cracked cover, the dog-eared corporality of the pages.

Later he met my American mother, fell in love, returned to the United States to declare his nuptial vows, procreate.

In 1983, a year after my birth, Twentieth Century Fox released the film *All The Right Moves*. This film became my father's point of reference for all things Real American: a bluesy dirge on the

American condition. Both beautiful and tragic, *All The Right Moves* carried its own quiet poetry in the filmic shots of flatlands littered with steel mills, like something out of D.H. Lawrence.

My family cast its net in suburbia, reeled in the accessories of upper-middle-class life: Japanese cars, cable TV, my own enrollment in a highly ranked public school. But as they built a particular America of their own, my father still held dear his Bicentennial/ Tom Cruise-inspired notion of Real America. He watched every single John Hughes movie, imagined himself substituted for the various romantic leads, dolled up for the prom, parting wavy hair in a grease-stained mirror, parting the virginal thighs of some midwestern beauty in the back of her father's Ford. It helped that my redheaded mother bore an uncanny resemblance to Molly Ringwald.

My father never attended a prom and will regret it—half-jokingly—for the rest of his life. I did attend a prom. There were no slow dances, or tender kisses, or hymens ecstatically untethered from their owners. I woke on a motel room floor with a massive hangover and the feeling that romance was a sham propagated by Hollywood.

So in a way—and maybe this is what I'm getting at—though I attended an actual prom, I still share my father's prom fantasy, the fantasy that life can be like a John Hughes film, that life can be like *Friday Night Lights, that there is such a place as Real America*. It is a harmless fantasy, but painful. It is painful because it illuminates the tragedy of American life: we will never live up to the myths we have created for ourselves.

In this, we are all Tim Riggins, looking longingly at the horizon. Yet my father and I (and my brother and mother, too) return always to tune in, set our gazes upon the immortal and infinitely rewatchable Dillon Panthers; we clear our eyes, and fill up our hearts, and hope against hope that the moment won't end. If that's not Real America, I don't know what is.

Really, Tim Riggins is Dillon, Texas: He's rough around the edges, but heartfelt and emotional in the center. He's often a giant mess in the macro sense, but he's always ready to do the right thing for the people he cares about. Dillon might be a hostile place to be if you're involved in the football culture, but the town itself is so unique in its sense of community and togetherness, even in the most difficult of times. So in the end, while everyone else decides to keep Dillon in their hearts, Tim does what he does best: Finds a new place to live inside Dillon's limits.

—**Cory Barker**, "Friday Night Lights 5.13 'Always' Review," TVOvermind.com

WHY WE LOVE

. . . Tim Riggins

Tim Riggins is damn sexy.

Actually, that doesn't quite do him justice. Let's try that again.

Tim Riggins is what raw sensuality looks like when it puts on a football jersey and maintains a blood alcohol content well above the legal limit. The tousled hair, the one-night-stand-in-the-bedroom eyes, that devil-may-care twang in his voice: these are the reasons female lust was invented.

Seemingly every woman in Dillon, Texas, with a functioning libido knows this, and Riggins takes full advantage of that fact. Hot high school chicks with stripper sisters, single moms with precocious sons, single bartender moms *and* their daughters, cheerleaders with strong Christian values—yeah, Riggins has hit all of that. And yet he most frequently returned to Lyla Garrity, that aforementioned responsible cheerleader, for reasons that should be obvious: she was the only girl in Dillon with a mouth as pretty as the one that sits right below Tim Riggins' pert and equally attractive nose.

But the fact that Billy Riggins' baby brother is smokin' hot, while certainly a notable fact, is not the reason we love Tim Riggins.

We love Tim Riggins because he's a drunken, often homeless fool who occasionally does the right thing. Because he's impulsive enough to celebrate buying a hydraulic lift at auction by following it up with the unnecessary purchase of a Texas longhorn steer.

Because he can wear plaid shirts and cowboy hats and still look like a sex god. And because he is willing to make a major sacrifice for his brother and his newborn nephew, even when no one tells him that he should. (Was there anyone during that end-of-season-four moment who wasn't screaming at their TV: "Don't do it, Tim. You don't deserve jail time. You need to remain a free, frequently fornicating man!")

In essence, we love Tim Riggins because when we ask ourselves WWRD—What Would Riggins Do?— sometimes the answer comes back: adopt a puppy on behalf of an essentially fatherless girl and name that little dog Skeeter.

There isn't enough room in this book to list all the reasons why we love this guy, so here are just a few.

- Tim Riggins is proof that drunkenness and football practice can occasionally, albeit unadvisedly, mix.
- Only Riggins would have the cojones—or, more accurately, the inebriated stupidity—to stand up at the Dillon Panthers roast and attempt this joke: "Hey, how about Matt Saracen sleeping with Coach's daughter?"
- Riggins is the kind of guy who still wants to believe in his dad, even when it's patently obvious he stole Coach Eric Taylor's video camera.
- Tim Riggins might not have appeared to be listening when Landry Clarke read *Of Mice and Men*, in its entirety, to him. But he still busted out a B-minus on his book report. And he even showed his appreciation by being the only guy who dared to applaud at Landry's Crucifictorious show.
- When the woman he loved decided to host a radio show that explored the faith she takes so seriously, he honored her religious commitment . . . by calling into the show, pretending

to be a girl named Tina from Waco, and confessing that Jesus is "so hot."

- After living with the ultracreepy Ferret Guy (and taking care of ferrets Roscoe and Coltrane), Riggins became the ultimate Fonzie to the Taylors' Cunninghams by briefly becoming their housemate. Con of this situation: he tried to drink their beer and watch their pay-per-view porn. Pro: he was the best big brother Julie never had.

- He can look at the rigorous schedule he's facing at daunting San Antonio State University and instantly recognize the profound lack of "me time."

- When action is needed on a friend's behalf—whether it's a trip to Mexico to talk Jason Street out of a risky surgery or an attempt to connect a confused and pregnant Becky with an adult who can give her sound advice—Tim comes through every time. And in the case of that Mexico trip, what we mean by "come through" can be summed up in two words: booze cruise.

- When Lyla Garrity told him she was going to pass on going to Vanderbilt University so she can stay at San Antonio State with him, Riggins looked her straight in the eyes and said: "Go."

- Riggins loves his brother, Billy. And he loves his nephew Stevie just as much, enough to look that newborn infant in the eye and lovingly say, "Stay angry."

- Only a guy as sexy as Tim Riggins could make cutesy behavior like mock-interviewing a dog with a beer can or carrying his little nephew still seem vaguely arousing.

- Riggins had the decency and class to let Becky down easy when the onetime ladies' man could have just as easily taken advantage of her for sex.

- Because Coach Taylor was right. There aren't many kids with more fortitude than the screwed-up, street-smart, hard-drinking, kindhearted, and, yes, smokin' hot Tim Riggins.

Riggins may not understand the premise of *The Scarlet Letter* ("It's about a gal named Scarlet, obviously," he once told Tami Taylor) but he is a multifaceted, flawed, often surprising character worthy of great literature . . . or at least a bodice-ripper about a hot guy who drinks a lot of Natty Bo.

The *Friday Night Lights* journey ended with Tim out of prison, swearing to remain an upstanding citizen and back where he belonged: on a wide-open piece of land, with a beer in his hand, possibilities in front of him and the warm Dillon breeze still blowing through that tousled hair. Texas forever? Sounds good to Tim Riggins.

WHY WE LOVE . . . Character Series from the *Washington Post*'s Jen Chaney

Class Not Dismissed

The Role of Economics and Money in the Story of *Friday Night Lights*

KEVIN SMOKLER

Friday Night Lights began its life as a true story and remained so until it landed on television. Published in 1990 as a book by Philadelphia journalist H.G. "Buzz" Bissinger, *Friday Night Lights: A Town, A Team, and A Dream* spanned the 1988 football season of the Permian High School Panthers in Odessa, Texas, and depicted the team's fanatical supporters. The book angered those supporters enough that not only did bookstores who featured it receive death threats, but Odessa itself barely cooperated with the 2004 film adaptation. *Friday Night Lights* the movie begins with the title card "the following is based on the 1988 West Texas Football Season" and uses the same team and player names. Odessa is never mentioned, and much of the movie was filmed in Abilene, Texas, three hours to the east.

When *Friday Night Lights* came to television in 2006, producer Peter Berg (who had also directed the film) changed the names of the characters and their high school, diversified the story line by placing women in more prominent roles, and dispensed with Odessa as a setting. The fictional Dillon is said to be "a few hours from Austin" and in "West Texas," which puts it somewhere around San Angelo and Abilene. Odessa is another three hours to the west of that, about seventy miles from the New Mexico border. *Friday Night Lights* the TV show was filmed in Austin and the surrounding hills, which is as far away geographically and culturally from Odessa as Detroit is from the hills of eastern Kentucky.

The road from book to big to small screen, or even between the latter two, is a treacherous one. On the shoulder you'll see as evidence the wreckages of failed movie-to-television-series such as *Ferris Bueller's Day Off* and *Back to the Future*, as well as television-to-movie travesties such as *Sex and the City 2*. The creative teams behind adaptations are under terrible pressure to give fans something new, but not so new they don't recognize the source material and not so derivative that the new thing seems like merchandising. The ones that succeed—*Happy Days, Mr. Belvedere, Buffy the Vampire Slayer*—are like great jazz covers: tones you recognize, other phrases you don't, but a thematic backbone that is both riffed on and always returned. For *Happy Days*, this backbone was nostalgia for youthful love and its comic possibilities. For *Mr. Belvedere*, it was understanding and compassion bridging national and class differences. For *Buffy*, it was the struggles of adolescence cast in gothic extremes.

Friday Night Lights has that backbone. Along the way from sports book to sports movie to one of the great television series of our time, its true north was class and economics. Class gives all three versions of *Friday Night Lights* their drama but also explains the changes made when it arrived on television—Dillon over Odessa, present versus past, and women as major characters. Class tells us why the show was filmed in Austin and why, unlike its antecedents, *Friday Night Lights* on TV is ultimately about hope on the other six days of the week.

Yes, *Friday Night Lights* is about "more than football." We've watched and know it is also about family, marriage, growing up, and life in a small town. But none of those are as thick a map line on *Friday Night Lights'* journey as class.

Let's trace it.

I. Place

Odessa/Dillon

The *Friday Night Lights* pilot begins much as the movie did: location shots at dawn, empty Texas fields and sky, a football stadium awakening with goal posts erected and lights turned on. And then the voice-over of a radio DJ . . .

> Good Morning, West Texas. Panther Football Radio 470 AM on your dial. It's Monday morning and we all know what that means. Only four days until Friday night, the night our Dillon Panthers bring the hammer down on the Westerby Mustangs.

. . . followed by a shot of Coach Eric Taylor walking onto the practice field wearing a jacket that says "Dillon Football."

The opening reminds us that we are in the world of movie and book—lonesome West Texas, fanatical about its high school football. But we haven't heard of this Dillon place, because it doesn't exist. We just know it's probably in the godforsaken middle of nowhere, much like Buzz Bissinger described Odessa in his book's opening chapters: "a land so vast, so relentless that something swells up inside, something that makes you feel powerless and insignificant." And yet in 1988 when Bissinger visited,

Odessa was not an isolated hamlet but a city of 90,000 people. Dillon may be big enough to support two high schools, but it feels about a quarter of that size. If Dillon ever had years of prosperity and growth, the television show implies, they were long ago and mostly forgotten. The town's better-off citizens (in new home construction with commodious front lawns) are small businesspeople like Buddy Garrity or educators like the Taylors. Most of the longtime residents—the families Riggins, Collette, and Saracen—live in shotgun houses or trailers on scruffy patches of earth. Dillon itself seems a place of hard luck with little redemption coming. Anyone who has grown up there and stayed is portrayed as pathetically grasping at past glory (Buddy, Billy Riggins) and unhappy and resentful because of it. Dillon's young people are already planning their escape.

Matt Saracen has his sights set on art school in one of the North's great metropolises, and only a sick grandmother would keep him around. Julie Taylor leaves for college, has a tough time of it, and ultimately ends up in Chicago, too. Tyra Collette, the seeming embodiment of a townie vixen, may always love Tim Riggins, but doesn't care about Dillon Panthers football. In the end she chooses to leave them both behind. Even the injured Smash Williams plays in triumph elsewhere, receiving a scholarship to Texas A&M.

The creators of *Friday Night Lights* have somewhat cruelly positioned Dillon as a town in paralysis whose healthy years go unmentioned. The series began with the promise of a new season and a potential state championship as the Dillon Panthers were led onto the field by star quarterback Jason Street, who had promised to come back home only in post-NFL triumph (he and Riggins toast to "Texas forever"). He wound up paralyzed a few minutes later. And though he spent much of seasons two and three around town, he eventually had a child, married, and moved to New York to become a sports agent. He did not return for the series finale. Even the local hero saw no future in staying local.

In his book, Bissinger makes a strong argument that young people seeing no future in Odessa is a relatively recent phenomenon. Odessa is a boom-bust town whose economic fortunes have been tied by baling wire to the price of oil in its surrounding fields. In good years, the city was a place of spacious homes, luxury cars, and locals growing up, starting businesses, and raising families there. In one particularly illuminating chapter, Bissinger widens the scope of his narrative beyond players and coaches and interviews. He interviews several dozen citizens of Odessa who have no connection to high school football save their fandom. Most declare the Permian Panthers give their lives meaning and their community pride. Some were sixty- and seventy-year-olds who haven't missed a game or a booster club meeting in forty years. While we can argue whether the intensity of that pride is both misplaced and harmful, these Odessans seem at peace with their choices. The young players may see their lives elsewhere (in the epilogue, Bissinger indicates most do leave town after graduation and don't come back). The older stalwarts will cheer just as loud next season.

Austin

Austin, Texas, won the rights to headquarter the cast and crew of *Friday Night Lights* the series in the early summer of 2006, both complicating and, in retrospect, making clear the force class and economics would assert on the story of a town, a team, and a dream. "This production will generate millions for the local economy," said Mayor Will Wynn to the *Austin Business Journal.* "It will give us the opportunity to further showcase our vibrant community and Texas for its love of football."

It might seem a rather parochial thing to say for a city that, in addition to being the state capital, is also a university town, the Silicon Valley of the south, and the "live music capital of the world," but make no mistake. Love of nonpro football is not some bizarre affectation that only happens in the Texas hinterlands. Austin is football crazy. UT Austin fans are said to "bleed burnt orange," and at the high school level the Westlake Chaparrals share a state record, a devoted fan base, and a former head coach with the Odessa Permian Panthers.

Odessa and Austin are also joined in a shared past that has as much to do with economics as football. The two cities are poetic representation of the two halves of a handoff of the Texas economy from industrial to information and from oil wells to microchips—a handoff that happened right before a journalist named Buzz Bissinger got to town.

In the fall of 1987, the "Black Monday" crash of the stock market (the single largest one-day decline in U.S. history) sent oil prices plummeting and the Texas economy (including Austin's) into a tailspin. Oil dependent cities like Odessa were hit worst of all. In a matter of months, businesses around Odessa closed by the dozen, and unemployment shot up. The football season covered in *Friday Night Lights* the book is exactly one year later, and the pressure on Permian to win state is doubly intense because of it. Without the inescapable shadow of an economy in ruins and poverty landing in Odessa like a sandstorm, it's easy to dismiss "the town" and "the dream" of Bissinger's book as forgettable fanatics with bad priorities, little different than the painted torsos and colored wigs the camera pauses on during Monday Night Football. Under that shadow, the score at the end of the fourth quarter on Friday Night is also the verdict on what the lives of Permian fans and Odessa's mean. Because deep down they feel that beyond the stadium lights, in the dark fields of the republic, they mean nothing.

Across the state and a few months before, something was happening in Austin. That spring, three newspapermen and a music booker founded South by Southwest, a small showcase of the region's music industry. Attracting national attention almost immediately, South by Southwest and the founding of Dell Computer Corporation (which began in Michael Dell's dorm room at UT Austin) around the same time served as lead blockers for Austin's transformation into the state's economic powerhouse and the first steps of the Texas economy into the twenty-first century information and service economy. Austin is now home to celebrities like Sandra Bullock and Matt McConaughey, athletes Lance Armstrong and Andy Roddick, and, most importantly for our purposes, filmmakers like Richard Linkater (whose debut film, *Slacker*, launched Austin into the mid-'90s zeitgeist) and Richard Rodriguez. In 2008, South by Southwest (now a music, film, and technology festival) became Austin's highest revenue special event adding $110 million to the local economy in a single week. *Friday Night Lights* at its peak brought Austin $33 million for an entire season.

The Austin Film Commission trumpets on its website that *MovieMaker* magazine has voted Austin "America's top city to shoot on location." The infrastructure that makes this so is a direct result of Austin's stable economy (mainly technology, buttressed by university and state government), tourism (mainly due to live music, festivals, and media attention thanks to factor No. 1), and a culture of filmmaking fertilized by No. 1 and No. 2. The *Friday Light Nights* crew wanted to shoot there; show creator Peter Berg and executive producer Jason Katims have said repeatedly that Austin's economic conditions are what made it possible. And when the show's tepid ratings in seasons two and three had its studio, Universal, questioning whether it could be shot for less money in New Mexico or Louisiana, Berg and his team balked. Apparently the best place for a television show about a dead-end Texas town was Texas' most prosperous city.

II. Past vs. Present

The 1988 Permian Panthers are now in their early forties. Mixing fact and fiction, their season is just a few years after the state champion team of Buddy Garrity, who is probably in his mid-to-late-forties. In the history of Texas football, those few years are the dividing line of a terrible before-and-after, during which the state and its teams personified the winning-means-everything zeitgeist of the 1980s.

Buddy Garrity's Dillon Panthers probably "won state" in the early 1980s, during what seemed like a Golden Age for Texas football. Dallas's Southern Methodist University had claimed a share of the college football national championship in 1981. The Dallas Cowboys won two division titles and five playoff spots between 1980 and 1985. The Texas A&M Aggies won the Cotton Bowl in both 1985 and 1987. All the while, the TV show *Dallas* reminded prime-time viewers that Texas—glittering sky-scrapers, gated mansions, and huge hair—held the spirit of the decade between its two long horns.

The year 1987 changed everything. That February, the NCAA voted to terminate the SMU football program because of rampant recruiting violations. And though the Permian Panthers won the state championship in 1989 and again in 1991, by the mid-1990s, the school's football program was in ruins, a losing record with players, boosters, and fans deserting in scores. In no small part due to the "wake-up call" and "medicine" of the publication of *Friday Night Lights* in 1990, being a fanatical Permian Panthers fan is no longer viewed as the birthright of every Odessan but rather something you more often "expressed under your breath." The team began wining district champion-ships again in 2005 but has not come close to "taking state" for nearly two decades.

When examined closely, the record of the Permian Panthers seems to track in eerie converse to the national economy: state championships in economic down years like 1972 and 1989; barren, losing seasons during the first dot-com boom. When examined this way, the dedication of Permian supporters seems a lot more fair weather than their booster club would like to admit. Fans love the Panthers more when they win (understandably), and the Panthers seem to do better when Odessa is doing worse.

The creators of *Friday Night Lights* the television show set the series in the present. This could reflect their awareness of the poor track record of recent television series set in the past (*Freaks and Geeks, American Dreams, Life on Mars*) or perhaps they didn't want to worry about everyone talking on wall phones and feathering their hair. Practical, financial, or otherwise, the present-dayness of the show is of a specific sort. None of the characters have iPhones or stalk each other on Facebook. Totems of popular culture are rarely mentioned, and there are no guest performances by popular-for-a-minute music groups. It's as if its creators wanted *Friday Nights Lights* suspended in an expired present, not quite then, but with now quickly leaving them behind. The television show also isn't saddled with the win-at-all-costs ethos of the 1980s. But what do its characters want? A winning season? Escape? Life outside Dillon? A job that pays? Simple requests some, others a complete fantasy. They all have one thing in common: an anywhere-but-here restlessness breathing the oxygen of a place going nowhere.

III. Characters

Friday Night Lights, both book and film, revolves around six football players and a head coach. Supporting characters—a loving wife here, an alcoholic father there—have a few key scenes but are largely peripheral. The book and the film are solar systems with eighteen-year-old boys dreaming of playing in the NFL as the planets.

On television, *Friday Night Lights'* character ecosystem showed a marked shift in priorities. Of the first six cast members who are also players, only Smash Williams ends up playing college ball. Matt Saracen and Tim Riggins never have any intention of doing so. (Riggins' offer at UTSA is unsolicited. He gets in, but also never shows up.) Vince Howard's and Luke Cafferty's character arcs seem balanced on an awakening of a future without football and football as training for, instead of a relief from, an adult life of self-sufficiency. The shattered gridiron dreams of Jason Street looms as an ominous warning over the entire series. Perhaps high school football is something to learn from and leave behind.

Nowhere is this clearer than in the show's troupe of female characters, all of whom have been arranged along a continuum of economic power and life options. At one end is Julie Taylor, who left Dillon, went to college, and sought a future of her own choosing—even if she temporarily returned after college scandal. At the other end are Mindy Collette and the mothers of Becky Sproles and Vince Howard, who all seem trapped in Dillon by lack of education, nonexistent career options, and poor taste in men. Nearest them is Becky, who seems either wedded to Dillon or headed for a future dependant on a man from Dillon. Closer to her daughter, Julie, is Tami Taylor, who begins the series as a wife and mother who follows her husband's job but ends it as an educator in her own right, one whose career ultimately determines her family's future. And floating between poles is Jess Merriweather, who moves to Dallas as matriarch to her family of brothers but does so as a female football coach in training.

The *Friday Night Lights* television team has chosen not only to have women occupy greater screen time than in the film, but also to have them anchor the issues at the show's spiritual center: a life well lived, outside of the limits of economic opportunity. Each actress' character arc is deeply tied to realizing her potential and contribution beyond how she looks or whom she cheers for or dates. Yes, Lyla becomes a Christian, Tyra witnesses a murder, and Jess struggles with her love of football and a football player, and sense of responsibility to the Lions as their student manager. But these challenges are mere speed bumps. The realizing of latent potential *Friday Night Lights* concerns its female characters with is very much an economic potential, of college, careers, and the freedom of not having to depend on someone you once loved but no longer respect.

IV. Hope

The tagline for *Friday Night Lights'* first two incarnations was "hope comes alive on Friday night." On television, it seems to be "hope comes from what you do the other six days of the week." And although much of the show's first season stays focused on the state championship fortunes of the Dillon Panthers, in subsequent seasons it places just as high a value on the struggles of daily existence. In giving *Friday Night Lights* its annual "Buffy Award" for Most Underappreciated Television, Salon.com held it up against a pop culture universe of "perky, overstyled, bantering professionals," by instead praising its concerns with "[r]eal Americans living regular lives, enduring the indignities of frustrating, dead-end jobs, grappling with narrow-minded co-workers or neighbors, ushering up laughter in spite of family arguments, and doing the best with what they have."

Rent, bills, passing English class, workplace, and local politics: these are dramatic bones of *Friday Night Lights*, but rarely are they featured on television drama as a species. In Dillon, they take on a special pathos thanks to the cultural dominance of Dillon Panther and East Dillon Lion games, which serve both as the relief from and a searchlight pointed at those struggles. Few of us watching have the same kind of love for high school football teams, and yet we care so deeply about the lives of the Taylor, Williams, Saracen, Garrity, Collette, Riggins, and Howard families, whether or not we care for the sport at the center of their lives at all.

The easy answer, of course, is to thank great casting, writing, and acting. And we should do that. But set *Friday Night Lights* down in Portland, Oregon, Madison, Wisconsin, or even Austin instead of Dillon, and we'd probably care a whole lot less. The citizens of those places inhabit municipal embodiments of a bright American future. They've got plenty to busy themselves with, to care about, to live for. That high school football is the highest priority in Dillon, Texas, is the sad, desperate air the characters of *Friday Night Lights* live under and breathe. It shows us, with quiet insistence, that this program, our program, is about football and family and life in an American town past its prime, yes, but its sorrow and beauty comes from economic and class desperation, something rarely seen on American television because it also happens to be America's favorite lie to tell to itself.

The show's pilot ends with the death of a promising football career. Jason Street's paralysis is a tragic reminder of what happens to a town that has placed everything on the athletic feats of an eighteen-year-old and then has nothing when they lie crushed at midfield.

As Jason lies critically injured in a hospital bed and his teammates, family, and friends wait sobbing in the waiting room, we hear a voice-over of Coach Taylor, speaking in prayer . . .

Give all of us gathered here tonight the strength to remember that life is so very fragile. We are all vulnerable and we will all at some point in our lives, fall. We will all fall. We must carry this in our hearts that what we have is special. That it can be taken from us. And when it is taken, we will be tested. We will be tested to our very souls.

It is perhaps the greatest and the most easily forgotten lesson we have to learn from sports: that sometimes we win, and sometimes we lose, but we always reenter the world after the game. That lesson that did not reach the *Friday Night Lights* of Permian and Odessa one autumn twenty-five years ago. That town and its team had a dream propped up by economic desperation—nothing mattered more than to "win state" because it was a substitute for not being able to win the daily struggle of life in America. *Friday Night Lights* on television seems to have learned from its source material that life is actually about a bigger challenge: how to rise above circumstance and the smallness of winning and losing—class-based or otherwise. How when someone else would like to define our town or our team as triumphant or passé, we speak instead for ourselves. And have the confidence and the hope that it will be heard and matter.

Where will we be without this one of a kind show; one that, in its unapologetic fondness for small town life as it is lived by millions of Americans, stood apart from so much of the rest of dramatic television? [*Friday Night*] *Lights* didn't need doctors, lawyers, detectives or crime scene investigators to keep its stories moving. Instead, it focused on the challenges faced by ordinary working class people for whom the simple pleasures were the best: family dinners, time spent with friends, town parades and especially Friday night high school football games. And it did so with so much grace and compassion that it transcended much of its medium—especially broadcast ...

[*Friday Night*] *Lights* debuted in 2006, and at the time it proved to be a much-needed reminder that not everyone in America had succumbed to the unprecedented greed and rampant consumer spending that was devouring so much of the country at the time, including the working class. That may be why it didn't register with a large audience. Who wanted to be reminded that ordinary folks like the residents of Dillon were still living in small homes, driving old cars and struggling to pay their bills while selflessly caring for their loved ones—not when there was so much money to spend and there were so many good times to be had and so many McMansions to be built? Then the economy went into the tank, and [*Friday Night*] *Lights* in its last two seasons suddenly reflected a newer and broader reality.

Ed Martin, "*Friday Night Lights*: A Fond Farewell,"
HuffingtonPost.com

WHY WE LOVE

. . . Jason Street

The game-changing moment in Jason Street's life—that spine-altering instant when he attempted a tackle and took a paralyzing hit—is the inciting incident for everything that followed on *Friday Night Lights*. But it was what Jason Street did after that horrible, life-altering moment that defined him and our opinion of him.

Even at his most despondent, his most bitter and most eager to (justifiably) punch Tim Riggins in the face, Jason is still the sort of person most of us hope, on our very best of days, to become. Through dedication and force of will, he invariably achieves some level of success at almost everything he chooses to do. Physical therapy, coaching Matt Saracen to be a better QB, selling cars, becoming a sports agent . . . heck, when he set his mind to it, he was even pretty talented at flipping houses.

Okay, maybe he didn't make the U.S. quad rugby team, but he managed to catch on to the game and excel pretty quickly—specifically, after only three episodes. He's pretty close to perfect, but he's such a nice guy, with such an all-American, earnest face, that the thought of resenting or disliking him doesn't even occur to anyone. He's Jason Street, all moral fiber and forgiveness and fine human being. If he weren't so affable and cool, he'd probably make us upchuck.

Street, while occasionally capable of cracking a solid joke, is not Captain Comedy. He's the dogged and determined Dillon Panther alumnus, the perpetual straight man to party-heartying cutups like Tim Riggins and Herc. But even this—laughing at their sarcastic comments—is something he's pretty good at. That's the kind of guy Jason Street is; he excels in the art of making others shine. Actually, in many ways on *Friday Night Lights*, that's the most important thing he did: he made other people better.

For that reason, as well as the reasons listed below, we love Jason Street.

- At a backyard party with friends, where his best bud, Tim Riggins, was knocking back beers even though they were in football-season mode, Jason Street drank nothing but limeade out of a can.

- When Coach Taylor clearly couldn't bear to consider a Panthers team without Jason Street, it was the bedridden QB1 who put on a smile through tears and told him how much he liked his replacement, Matt Saracen. "If you free him up out there," Street said, "he'll make some things happen for you." That is what pure class looks like.

- When Jake, the boy who lived next door to the Streets, asked Jason if he could walk, he politely said no. Then he raced him, wheelchair against bike, and capped it off by reminding the kid he shouldn't play in the street. That bell you heard ringing at the end of this scene? That was the sound of angel Jason Street earning what had to be his 187th pair of wings.

- Despite his aforementioned role as perpetual straight man, Street developed an admirable sense of humor about his disability. Example: after listening to Smash and Riggins complain about their girl problems, he quipped: "Chair says I win."

- When his parents filed a lawsuit against Dillon High and Coach Taylor, Jason was the only one with enough of a moral compass to suggest they settle for a modest amount that covered the family's debts and mortgage. How did he even know how much that was? Because he's Jason Street, and that means he has his finger on the pulse of the family's finances and a set of ethics as straight as a ruler's edge.

- Despite the fact that Tim Riggins failed to visit him in the hospital after he got hurt, slept with his girlfriend, and got arrested when they traveled to Mexico, Jason still considers him his best friend. Texas forever? Hell yes.

- He may be all serious and earnest, but don't kid yourself: if Jason Street goes to a karaoke bar in Mexico and has a few cervezas, he will put on a hat and sing "La Cucuracha."

- If Jason is on a date with someone he met on the internet, he will not hesitate to flee if the girl mentions that what gets her going is "pee." This might be the only rude thing Street has ever done.

- Jason being Jason, that one rude thing wound up scoring him a one-night stand with a waitress (Erin) and eventually— courtesy of an unexpected pregnancy—a wife.

That unexpected pregnancy gave Jason something he thought, after his injury, he might never get: a son. And it was that son who prompted him to finally leave Dillon, Texas, to walk away from the place filled with memories of his football promise and build a new life for himself.

Jason and Erin named their baby boy Noah, which happens to mean the same thing as the Sanskrit word that Street got tattooed on his arm in Austin: peace. By the end of *Friday Night Lights*—after all the physical therapy and the lawsuits, the broken relationships and dreams destroyed—Jason Street finally found exactly that.

Quarterback Jason Street . . . isn't merely a good arm, though—he's a natural leader, wholesome and good-natured.

That's why, when Jason takes a hard blow in the first game and is carried away on a stretcher, unable to move or feel his limbs, we know more has been taken from this team than its quarterback, or its chance of making it to state. These boys have lost their moral center. Their heart.

—**Dyana Herron**, "So Long, *Friday Night Lights*," ImageJournal.org

WHY WE LOVE

. . . Herc

Herc has no last name. We've never heard Jason Street or anyone else refer to it. It's not listed on imdb.com, or on any *Friday Night Lights* wiki pages. Basically, the wheelchair-bound smartass and Jason's two-time roommate is like Prince or Oprah: he's such a legend, one word is all he needs.

He's Herc: the guy who got to know his new rehab roommate by sticking his fingers in his scrambled eggs and ogling the female friends who came to visit.

Herc: a dude who can never resist a par-tay.

Herc: a loyal friend to Jason Street who is so incapable of hiding his dislike of Lyla Garrity, he actually booed when he found out Street had gotten back together with her.

Herc: the quad rugby player who knows how to fire up his teammates.

Herc: someone who always tells it like it is, with no words minced and no trace of sugarcoating.

Herc: a disabled man with so much sass, energy, and attitude that he seems anything but disabled.

For his candor, confidence, and, perhaps above all else, his ability to crack us up every time he wheels his way into the *Friday Night Lights* picture, we love Herc. And because we love him, we know the best way to honor him is with a list of his best *Friday Night Lights* quotes.

- "I knew you had some fight in you." —After ramming his wheelchair into his new roommate's chair and screaming at him until finally Jason throws a glass of water at him
- "For a while, I wanted to go back to the hospital. Of course, that was partially because there was this hot-ass nurse who just could not get enough of me." —On adjusting to life after his accident
- "Of course your ding-dong went soft. It was trying to protect you." —Explaining to Jason why his attempt to have sex with Lyla was unsuccessful
- "You listen to me, grasshopper. There's going to be a million Buddy Garritys out there who will try to tell you you aren't worth anything. And you've just got to look him right in the eye and flip him the bird." —Telling Jason how to respond to Buddy's confession that he doesn't want Lyla to spend her life caring for a disabled man. He follows up this comment by smiling and doing his version of flipping the bird— holding up the curled fingers on his paralyzed hand.
- "Let me ask you: are you trying to be a cliché? Stem cell surgery in Mexico? Oh, let me check my watch: yep, been about a year. You're actually right on time for the miracle surgery portion of the show." —On Jason's plan to walk again by exploring surgery
- "Beta carotene—that's good for you, isn't it?" —Making like Eddie Haskell after Jason's mom brings the boys a snack of carrot sticks
- "Dude, you do not have to hide porn from a baby. Babies are not freaked out by boobies . . . babies love vaginas. They just took a great trip through one. It's like looking at a post-card." —After Jason throws away Herc's nudie magazines before baby Noah arrives

- "You don't know Burt Bacharach? Why am I here with him?"
  —To Billy Riggins after an argument about removing the retro wood accents from the house they just purchased
- "I'm thinking about one of two things: either open up an orphanage or b., I'm going to go ahead and see how many margaritas I can buy with fourteen grand." —On what he plans to do with his portion of the profits from flipping Buddy Garrity's house

Just before Jason Street proposed to Lyla, he explained how much Herc had inspired him, so much so that he wanted to do the thing that Herc would do in the situation.

"He would dump me and go after Tyra," Lyla said. "He would. He told me."

That's Herc in a nutshell right there: admirable and inspiring, but also willing to tell a woman, to her face, that he'd ditch her in favor of a hot blonde chick. God bless him for that.

Like that other classic of small-town America, *It's a Wonderful Life*, [*Friday Night Lights*] is about community, its benefits and its burdens. Coach Taylor, like George Bailey, is put upon, second-guessed and sometimes held back by his town . . .

Yet when he's tempted to quit or when college-coaching opportunities come along, he's drawn back by the people who need him: the kids for whom football is their shot at college, the locals who hold to their team with a faith akin to theirs in God . . .

It's not only Coach Taylor who feels the tug of others. Story line after story line on [*Friday Night Lights*] is about having responsibility for someone else.

—**James Poniewozik**, "Farewell to *FNL*: Bridging
America's Divides," Time.com

The knowledge that "Clear Eyes, Full Hearts, Can't Lose" is something you can learn—that it doesn't have to be inborn—is the reason we love this show: that we can, in our daily lives, live with this kind of integrity and openness to whatever the world offers us, and not feel ashamed or naïve; that it is better to live with an open heart that allows us to believe in the possibility of an impossibly long pass, and the love of two people that endures no matter what; that the love of a show about football in Texas has nothing to do with football or Texas, and is instead about the potential each of us has to be normal, regular, incredible people—that's what's been given to us.

—**Duana**, "Clear Eyes, Full Hearts, Can't Lose," LaineyGossip

The Drama of Being Decent

PAULA ROGERS

Every kid who has ever wondered why she has to spend her time wearing itchy pants and running around after a ball always hears the same words as her parents shove her up to the plate (or what have you): sports build character. They teach you how to be a decent, selfless person.

Just look at how the language of sports is used in daily life. Being a good sport means putting up with what you know to be bunk for the benefit of others around you. Another way of saying that is to be "game." Sportsmanlike conduct is honorable and fair. Someone who reports on bad behavior is a tattler, unless that behavior is truly corrupt. Then they're lauded as a whistle-blower. Okay, I'm getting a flag on the out-of-bounds use of the word "score." But still, the tally adds up to a linguistic slamdunk: the value of sports is in teaching us how to rise above petty ego and make efforts for the good of a group.

So, it's not a new idea that sports are about teamwork. But *Friday Night Lights* is a show about sports that runs with those same noble virtues *off* the field. Its plots explore just how rewarding it can be to take the high road and make the right choice, not just for your own benefit, but also for the benefit of others. And that focus explains the appeal of *Friday Night Lights* to many of its viewers. The show models a type of living and a kind of human purpose that we instinctively want to be around: simple goodness.

The Invisible Choice

Beyond the drama of each big game, the main conflict of the show lies in how every one of the main characters is just trying to do what's right. No one is scheming, and no one is stirring up poison apples in the locker room. Who is the villain in Dillon? Even when the Panthers/Lions lose a game, the only villain is simply life: the brutal fact that sometimes that's just how it goes.

Week after week, *Friday Night Lights* explored the consequences of the honest mistake and the impact of the small gesture. The characters have flaws but few truly depraved vices. Most wrongs that occur (taking steroids, sleeping with your paralyzed best friend's girlfriend, committing murder) can be traced back to sincere motives (pressure to succeed and support your family, love, defense of a friend in danger). The problems are soapy and even somewhat standard, but somehow the plots never tip over into the typical dramatics.

That feeling of narrative restraint prevails because of where the actions taken to right those worldly wrongs mostly take place: in living rooms and locker rooms, and occasionally at Applebee's. In fact, there are not so many grand actions taken in *Friday Night Lights* as there are grand words offered. The central issues of the show have very high stakes, like addiction, abuse, and neglect. Yet even the most severe of transgressions very rarely leads to the inside of any kind of system, legal or otherwise. Even when Tim

Riggins was sent to jail, it was an act of self-sacrifice so that his brother could be with his wife and new baby, despite being more responsible for the actual crime. The plot was less about Tim doing the time than it was about the reasons why he goes to prison. In fact, we never saw Tim behind bars unless he was being visited by people who wanted to help him. Watching Tim suffer mattered less in the world of the show than his great act of bravery, because *Friday Night Life* extols the virtues of selfless acts of kindness.

Tim's prison plot point was "simple goodness" in a dramatic nutshell. It was one person deciding to personally step in and take action on behalf of someone else. It was a refusal to let anyone end up lost to the cold machinations of society, even if it would be easy to just look the other way. When this simple goodness is enacted on a community-wide scale, as it was in Dillon, it forms a safety net made up of individual acts of kindness that prevents anyone from falling too far out of control. With this principle guiding each character, no problem is so big that it can't be solved with the salve of sincere concern and heartfelt wisdom. Whether in West or East Dillon, whether it's Coach Taylor having to counsel a player or friends owning up to letting each other down, the ultimate solution offered is the humility to have a tough conversation. Dramatic climax on *Friday Night Lights* usually involves a doorbell.

But in the show as it is in life, simple goodness—doing the right thing—is actually a much more difficult way to deal with problems. For one, it's an all-or-nothing arrangement—because people start to depend on decency. Dillon's resident "Good Man," Eric Taylor, is a clear example of that. It's a funny quirk to the culture that his first name has essentially been replaced with "Coach" to the people of Dillon, but it reflects the character's personal choice, as well. He is never off the field. He takes his responsibility to heart, assuming the role of guardian to his players as soon as they join his team.

Yet this role gets complicated from the first episode by Jason Street's sudden paralysis. As the dreams of the star quarterback, the team, and the town were in shambles, Coach had no option but to act to save his career, sure. But the method he chose was not grandstanding or blaming or moving away. He chose to open his heart to the players, specifically Matt Saracen, and nurture a potential that could only be coaxed forth through personal attention and kindness. Then, once he had begun to shepherd one young player, others noticed and started to depend on him, as well. In the show's full arc we saw Eric mentor, among others, Tim, Landry Clarke, Smash Williams, and Vince Howard, and even continue helping Jason. Maybe this was more than he bargained for, but his role had been solidified in the town as soon as he started helping Matt. Episode after episode, Eric shows that a reputation for kindness becomes an open invitation for anyone dealing with the distinct lack of kindness we see too often in the world.

As the action moved to East Dillon, Coach Taylor had the opportunity, if he wanted it, to recast himself as more of an all-business type with the new team. But of course he did the exact opposite. He became even more personally invested in his under-privileged new team, and even turned down a lucrative job offer coaching college in Florida for the chance to make an impact on his high school team's lives.

But the generosity of spirit doesn't stop with Eric when it comes to the Taylors. Tami Taylor also echoes her husband's "pillar of the community" role. Tami offers great support and counsel to her husband from the very first episode, but in her role as guidance counselor and eventually as principal at West Dillon High, Tami starts to extend her sage advice beyond the realm of her marriage and steers many a student straight. With the move to East Dillon, she adopts the tireless guardian role for herself in earnest, giving sincere advice to teens like Becky

Sproles and Epyck Sanders even when it threatens both her career and personal safety. By season four, Eric and Tami have become personal caretakers for many of the town's young people, making them a kind of power couple of good old-fashioned wisdom. But the efforts pay off for both Taylors. He eventually led his team of the kids nobody wanted to a state championship, and she got offered a job as dean of admissions at a fancy East Coast college. Simple goodness, *Friday Night Lights* suggests, benefits the giver as much as it does the receiver, even if it is very time-consuming.

But one other tough thing about doing "the right thing" is that it's often extremely quiet. Coach Taylor might be in the spotlight for how his team performs on Friday night, but there was no talk radio play-by-play the morning after he took Matt under his wing, or when he made house calls to keep Smash from self-destructing. And isn't it braver to do the right thing when no one is watching? There's no applause to soak up after making the tough choice; instead there's only the self-sacrifice that comes from making it. Coach Taylor does earn the thanks and respect of the people he helps, but at the end of the day his job is judged on how many games he wins, not how many hearts.

Of course the construct of a television show is that any hidden acts of noble character do not go unseen. Each moment is seen by the audience, if not the town. The fact that we are silent witnesses to these small acts of bravery makes them all the more affecting, because it produces an unconscious need in us to vouch for them. We root for the characters all the more because as the only people who've seen them do something good, it's almost our duty to see that they get their good karma. That's also why it's so moving when they do reap the rewards, because it feels like our victory, too. The drama of this simple goodness is what's resonated so deeply with viewers, creating a kind of community of people who want to believe in the right, if difficult or unpopular, choices.

The Pump Fake

That sense of community is, of course, echoed on the streets of Dillon. When characters do mess up, the support network is strong and generous. The town seems to have a code that knocking on doors to come in and chat is more appropriate than an email or a phone call. Neighbors look out for each other and cheer each other on in the big game, despite mistakes that might have been made in the days leading up to Friday night. More smarty-pants characters like Tyra or prefootball Landry occasionally make comments about how the only way to fit in within Dillon is to be a football hero. But after five seasons, I don't buy that simple assessment. If anything, football merely serves as a tidy excuse for these people to openly love each other in ways that can't be explained by modern social rules.

Ex-football star Buddy Garrity is forever plowing his way into the lives of the people he cares about under the guise that it's all about the game. First, it was Jason Street. After Jason's injury, Buddy seemed utterly heartless in urging his daughter to move on with a new love. He discouraged Jason from being involved with Lyla with appalling righteousness, telling a paralyzed young man that he could no longer offer any decent prospects. Yet despite his gestures toward steely pragmatism, Buddy never gave up on his feelings for Jason, or on the young man himself. Buddy helped Jason get a job at his car dealership, even though Jason wasn't very good at it. Buddy justified the move by extolling Jason's skills as quarterback and their natural translation into sales. But it was too late. Viewers could sense the real affection behind the excuse of athletic admiration, especially when those sales never materialized.

This shell game of loving people, er, football is a classic move from Buddy throughout the show, nicely carried through to the final season. During Tim Riggins' parole hearing, Buddy butted in to deliver what we expect will be an overblown speech made mostly for the purpose of convincing Eric to stay in Dillon, not getting Tim out of jail. Yet his rambling emotion managed to communicate more about the depth of Tim's character than Eric's stoic wisdom. There was a moment in the delivery of the speech where actor Brad Leland showed the character going for broke in a way that even surprised Dillon's seasoned pitchman. Buddy was suddenly talking about real emotion; he was showing his own heart in order to illustrate Tim's. He may have couched his presence in the interest of impressing Eric and keeping Dillon football strong, but the sweet, sappy truth of his love for Tim was evident as soon as he began to speak. It was Buddy's statement that seemed to tip the scales in Tim's favor.

Even the characters who are able to give love openly are more able to accept it under the comfort of the football dynamic. Jess Merriweather showed herself to be a very generous young woman. She took care of her brothers for her dad, helped out in his greasy restaurant, coached Luke when Vince flaked, and was generally sweet. When she was having a hard time with her break-up with Vince and the mounting pressures of her home life, she headed to the Lions' locker room to be by herself and fold towels and cry for a little while. But she wasn't alone. Coach Taylor saw her, and although Jess put on a brave face during what must have been her complete mortification at being caught crying in the locker room, he couldn't leave her pain unacknowledged. This moment led to one of the most touching lines of the whole series: his simple, "You know I have two daughters, don't you?"

This was also a tough time for Coach, as he faced Julie being back at home after some spectacularly bad choices in college. If football was merely his escape from domestic problems, he might have ignored Jess or admonished her about crying in football territory. But football isn't an escape from emotional difficulties; it's a way to deal with them. It's an easy language to learn for talking through tough times that really don't make much sense, no matter how you look at them. Jess received some comfort during a tough time, and Coach was able to reaffirm the father role he was struggling with at home. These two characters would never have had their respective healing moments without the common purpose of football to not only bring them together, but to provide a safe cover for touching on real emotion in a relationship that didn't otherwise allow that dynamic.

The final moments of the series finale beautifully illustrate the way in which the town's obsession with football is just another medium for love. The state championship was down to the wire, and Vince threw a classic Hail Mary pass to win the game. As the ball sailed through the night sky, we watched a series of close-ups on the Dillon audience, with everyone's eyes transfixed upward to see if Vince's pass would connect. Then we cut to Philadelphia, and it took a while before we saw the ring on Vince's finger and the 2010 State Champions banner on the Lions former field letting us know that they did win. We didn't see the actual catch and the actual moment of victory because those moments weren't what mattered. It was the collective dreaming and passion of everyone there, waiting and watching and hoping for the best together.

Football gives the people of Dillon a shared goal to see each other succeed. But as the characters prove off the field, that goal is actually about a lot more than scoring touchdowns.

Texas for Never

So if everyone in Dillon is just good, good, good, not to mention very good-looking, how can we stand to watch these saints? Probably because no matter how much we love the stories in Dillon, no one actually wants to live in Dillon.

The people in this version of small-town America may be lovely, but the landscape itself is not romanticized at all. The place is mostly a desolate, muggy-looking handful of modest houses, dirt patches, and ramshackle strip malls. Tim's land occasionally provides some shots of the beautiful Texas hill country, but the actual town of Dillon seems pretty sparse aesthetically and culturally. The aforementioned Applebee's played a recurring role in the early seasons as the main hub for emotional revelations, business discussions, employment, and a decent meal. Buddy's new bar has threatened Applebee's casual dining monopoly, but looks like it's made up of the exact same décor (an aesthetic *The Simpsons* has forever coined in my mind as "a lotta crazy crap on the walls"). The most elaborate architecture in town appears to be the pillars flanking the entrance to The Landing Strip. The characters don't frequent quaint little mom-and-pop shoppes or stroll down charming avenues untouched by corporate culture. They shop at Walmart, saddle up to small, sweaty picnic tables inside and outside of Ray's BBQ, and chat barely out of the splash zone of the deep fryer at the Alamo Freeze. Legitimate employment is scarce and limited to low-paying jobs at the high school, in retail, or in food service—usually involving a humiliating uniform of some kind. Or there's always The Landing Strip. The nearby Cafferty farm is not romanticized, either. Between Luke's injury and recurring responsibilities to fix fences and handle livestock, the simple life is shown to be a lot of hard work. It's not a glamorous look at rural Texas, but it is very realistic.

Yet ratings have shown that *Friday Night Lights* has one of the most affluent audiences on television. This is evidence of a large disconnect between the lives of the characters and the lives of the viewers, even beyond the usual prime-time gap between impossibly beautiful doctors and the actual people watching them at home. Clearly none of the main characters in Dillon are anything approaching wealthy. The only ostensibly well-off people are quickly shown to be poor in other ways, as with the morally bankrupt McCoys. Keeping the characters anchored in the low-to-middle economic classes helps offset their endless reserves of kindness. If the Taylors and the rest of the Dillon community had the monopoly on both strong community values and cozy upper-class lifestyles, it might make the show a bit nauseating to watch.

But *Friday Night Lights* is not about extolling Victorian notions of the noble poor. It's about showing the small-scale dignity that's possible in real life, even under less-than-ideal circumstances. Knowing that the characters struggle with tough moral choices alongside pressing practical concerns like college tuition or paying for housing makes the show's modest core values that much more earnest. So much of television responds to the drudgery of daily life by glazing over it with fluff or setting up elaborate distractions in gawking at the wealthy. *Friday Night Lights* does the exact opposite by making Dillon obviously a little run-down and a little bit of a dead end. Most viewers watching the show live in places that are nicer than Dillon, at least on the surface. So it follows that if simple goodness can prosper there and make it a livable town, it can be entirely feasible and perhaps even more powerful in the average modern locale with the average modern conveniences.

It's also important to the balance of the show's message that it doesn't use the physical or economic limitations of Dillon as a way to glorify the nostalgic American Dream or explain the decency of its residents. Small-town life isn't shown to be any more or less immune to human folly than life in a suburb or a city. In fact, for all their invaluable personal growth, most of the young main characters are desperately trying to get out of Dillon. Their failure to do so is always associated with dashed potential and compromise. The show makes sure that although these characters have had the basic misfortune to be born in a place with relatively little advantages, they don't simply become bitter or lazy. Like the emotional injustices they encounter, the teenage characters on *Friday Night Lights* conquer their physical circumstances and improve their situations through hard work and motivation. That ability is fueled by the sense of community and the more physical equivalent of that basic neighborly decency—the ability to rise above disadvantages of circumstance with dignity and determination.

The show is fiction that chooses real life, if perhaps a little more meager-than-average life, as its setting. We can get the comfort of being around good, decent types, something that's missing from most TV and perhaps most real-life days, without the show becoming cloying or predictable because the characters are not insulated in mansions and coziness. So the show illustrates the benefits of simple goodness in the lives of Dillon's residents as a main theme, but it also goes a little further. The writers ground those characters in a comparatively run-down place like Dillon so we can more easily picture taking that same simple goodness out into our own lives.

The Ties Won't Bind

As much as we love *Friday Night Lights*, it's hard to ignore that in almost every episode, almost every conflict is resolved in some way by the Taylors. Yet this consistent device is remarkably satisfying, even while it is predictable. We actually want the Taylors to emerge with the right solution, again and again. We actually cheer when they are shown to be almost comically perfect, no matter what is thrown their way. Part of the appeal of these characters is the deep and nuanced acting from Connie Britton and Kyle Chandler that shows inner conflict even while their speech and actions always project the right thing. But there is another force at work to complicate their sincerity just enough to keep the show from crystallizing into pure sugar: Julie Taylor.

As the daughter of modern TV's absolute model of healthy parenting, Julie had the best possible influences growing up, so far as the show has established. Yet she is the most selfish character, and the one who is the most oblivious to how her actions affect others. Even Buddy Garrity changed his tune to occasionally hum a few bars of humility after the traumas of his affair, losing his relationships with his children and falling into financial ruin.

Julie's obnoxiousness was a disturbing slow build. She was surprisingly comfortable flirting with another guy while dating dear, sweet Matt. Her fights with Tami were frustrating and petty, even if they painted an incredibly respectful portrait of teen angst. But in the final season, her already casual relationship with morality was definitely going through a rough patch. Julie slept with a married man, repeatedly, and was publicly shamed by his distraught wife. In the aftermath, Julie leaned on other people for support in increasingly desperate ways, from dropping out of school to intentionally wrecking her car to running away to find Matt in Chicago. But Julie was not seeking out her loved ones so they could help her figure out the right thing to do. Tami and Eric clearly spelled out what that would have been. Julie was greedily clinging to others just so they could make her feel better. (Even Matt saw through that one.) She was simply too ashamed to return to school after her transgression played out in front of her whole dorm. Beyond her seeming confusion between the inner workings of a dorm and a convent, it's interesting that a young woman who grew up watching her parents systematically forgive and heal the townspeople one-by-one would find it so impossible to forgive and heal herself.

Julie's tailspin added a crucial caveat to the show's message about the power of kindness. Namely that character can't be inherited; it has to be earned. If every member of the Taylor family were perfect, the show would simply be about the ease of moral privilege. Eric and Tami's eternal wisdom had to be foiled by their own daughter's blind spot to the same kind of integrity they've fostered in criminals, alcoholics, broken heroes, and other lost souls who have come under their guidance. This keeps them human and relatable, making sure they don't seem simply more evolved than the other characters who struggle with pain and loss. In that case they would be more like leaders of an orphanage rather than kind people in a community. This crack in the Taylors' veneer was heartbreakingly demonstrated when Julie moved back home after ditching college, and Eric struggled to even look at his own daughter because he couldn't relate to her selfish choices. The show had to prove that the Taylors could personally handle the same kinds of problems that they help others navigate. After all, it's much easier to dole out words of advice than it is to follow them. In giving Tami and Eric a legitimate challenge in their own lives, the show let us trust that they not only have the wisdom to see the right thing, but the character to actually do it.

In the end, it was the pressure to do right in front of their daughter, who openly admits that she sees them as her role models, that pushed both Tami and Eric to confront the biggest issue in their marriage with selfless hearts. It's completely touching that both Taylors take on this responsibility independently and come to two different, self-sacrificing conclusions. Both Eric and Tami win in the end, with two good jobs and a marriage that's stronger than ever, but it's been proven, once and for all, that these two can do more than just talk the talk. Without Julie, watching every down-and-out kid (and adult) in Dillon make their way to the Taylors' doorstep one night for an unannounced S.O.S. would be an uncomfortable display of superiority. With her, the show tarnishes its heroes just enough to illustrate that the real work is not just in doing the right thing, but earning the judgment to understand what the hell that is.

Why Can't They Lose?

Clear eyes. Full hearts. The art of *Friday Night Lights* is in how it makes you feel good after you watch it—not smug, smart, superior, or even refreshed after a good dose of turning your brain off and just soaking in the glow. By showing sincerity as a complicated and brave choice, *Friday Night Lights* validates it as a modern choice. I can't have been the only fan who has walked away from the TV fantasizing about what Tami or Coach Taylor would advise in my own personal life drama. I just imagine a pair of crinkled sincere eyes under a worn baseball hat, or a warm voice calling me honey, and I'm motivated by the idea that honesty really can sort things out. That's an endangered notion to take into the world, but one that is empowering exactly because of its rarity (even if it turns out to be an imperfect mantra). We all know that being a decent person is often a day-to-day (or sometimes hour-by-hour) choice. The Taylors and the characters of Dillon become something like allies in navigating a complicated world through good intentions.

Friday Night Lights is high-minded in a way that no other hour of TV can be without airing on PBS or ending with a 1-800 number to call and donate. The show's message is that simple human decency is not only possible, but also extremely valuable. First of all, *Friday Night Lights* proves that nice people can be very compelling in a smart TV drama, and hopefully that will be used to nudge the bar a little higher for a genre nearly lost to cads and cadavers. But, in the moral-of-the-story sense, *Friday Night Lights* illustrates exactly what decency can accomplish. Basic goodness won't save you from tricky circumstances or unfair losses. But it is the only way to build anything resembling a community, because it generates the electric current of all human relationships: trust.

It's trust that invites viewers in to Dillon on a deeper level than they are invited into any other TV town or bar or home, and trust that leaves us with a takeaway beyond entertainment. As fans invested in the characters, we know that even when bad things happen to good people, it isn't going to make them stop being good. In fact, it might even make them better. That basic narrative guideline makes the show a great comfort to watch while we each take a break from our own lives, hoping that when we get back to reality we can find a way to make the best of whatever comes our way.

WHY WE LOVE (to Hate)

. . . Joe McCoy

Almost every character on *Friday Night Lights* could justifiably be described as a good person. Every character, that is, except for one: Joe McCoy.

Joe McCoy is the ultimate entitled, demanding asshole father. We're not saying he's the root of all evil *necessarily*, but he certainly bears a strong resemblance to it. That's right: evil wears a button-down shirt, perpetually sports a know-it-all look on its face, has a pseudo-mullet for a haircut, and, occasionally, drives a golf cart.

Oh, and those reading glasses? Joe McCoy didn't need them to read. He wore them solely to emphasize his ability to look down his nose at other people.

The writers of *Friday Night Lights* dared to introduce this character in the midst of the U.S. economic recession, at a time when arrogant rich guys seemed even more villainous than usual. And we're convinced that, as a result, during several episodes from the third and fourth seasons of *Friday Night Lights* an untold number of TV sets had to be replaced after irate fans put their fists through the screen, just hoping they might connect with Joe McCoy's chin and finally knock out that smug, wealthy mo-fo once and for all. Of course, the purchase of all those new TVs only helped corporate America. So once again, the rich guys won. Damn you, Joe McCoy. Damn you to *hell*.

We hated this man so much, in fact, that, by extension, we grew to hate everyone in his family. At first, we felt sorry for J.D., the innocent and clearly talented Panther who was forced to deal with his dad's diabolical need to build him into a football god. But then J.D. turned into a punk who looked down his nose—without the aid of reading glasses, mind you—at the East Dillon Panthers and acted just as self-entitled as Daddy had always taught him to be. What's that saying? The douchebag doesn't fall far from the tree?

And as for Joe's wife, Katie, we actually kind of liked her until she told Tami she wanted nothing to do with her after that whole incident with Child Protective Services. We understood where Katie was coming from, but still, no one talks to our Tami like that. Especially someone who at some point clearly had the thought: *Hey, Joe McCoy seems like a nice man; I bet he'd make a solid husband.*

We love to hate Joe McCoy because he stands in such stark opposition to everyone else in his Dillon, Texas, orbit. In a sea of Matt Saracens and Eric and Tami Taylors—people trying with all their hearts to be decent and right—Joe McCoy is a colossal ass who doesn't even bother disguising his own assiness. And for that, as well as the noted reasons below, we love to hate that @&#!ing son of a @&#!.

- After sending a Juicy Brothers smoothie truck onto the field in the middle of practice, Joe waltzed into Eric Taylor's office to apologize with a juicy bribe: a Cuban cigar and a bottle of scotch. He also didn't hesitate to mention that Coach had a franchise in J.D. McCoy sitting under his nose; all he had to do, Joe said, was sniff. Oh, Coach Taylor sniffed. And he definitely smelled something.
- In addition to controlling his son's free time and how he played on the football field, Joe McCoy also dictated the

terms of his son's love life, forcing him to dump Madison—possibly the last girl who would ever genuinely like J.D., since he turned into a mega-d-bag not long after.

- It was bad enough that Joe McCoy punched his own child in the face. But he did it in an Applebee's parking lot, which is just tacky behavior unbecoming of someone who lives in a McMansion. And the fact that he did it after the Panthers won a game that would take them to state? Well, that was just stupid.

- Joe McCoy is the sort of person who thinks he can start recruiting for the Dillon Panthers simply because he has "backed up a truckload of cash" for the team. He's also the sort of person who will point out that he's backed up a truck-load of cash for a team.

- McCoy not only used his Machiavellian ways to get Eric Taylor fired as coach of the Dillon Panthers, he had him replaced with his son's personal coach, Wade Aikman. He replaced Eric with a man named *Wade*. We don't think we need to explain all the things that are wrong with that.

- God, we love to hate Joe McCoy most of all for that maddening smirk on his face when Tami Taylor was booed at an assembly for her decision to send Luke Cafferty to East Dillon High. That self-righteous, outrageous little smirk. Just makes a person want to punch him right in his obnoxious, square-chinned . . . oh, crap. There goes the TV screen.

Joe, his wussy son J.D., and their fancy-pants house were notably absent from the final episodes of the *Friday Night Lights*. Weirdly, we kind of missed them. Because even on a show about the inherent goodness of humanity, sometimes don't you just want somebody to loathe?

WHY WE (Mostly) LOVE
. . . Julie Taylor

very *Friday Night Lights* fan adores the Taylor family. Who could resist Tami, the compassionate yet firm mother with the open mind and loving heart? Or Eric, the devoted, football-obsessed yet sensitive man of the house? Or even that darling, frequently absent little Gracie Belle Taylor?

And then there's . . . Julie Taylor.

Don't get us wrong. We love Julie. We do. It's just that sometimes, well, we didn't like her very much. It's not her fault, really. We blame the affliction that frequently plagued Julie Taylor throughout the course of *Friday Night Lights*, an affliction known as . . . being a teenage girl.

If you're the parent of a teenage girl, or the teacher of teenage girls, or if you've merely come across a teenage girl while running errands at the local strip mall, you know how they are. They're smart-mouthed, stubborn little women determined to wear revealing clothes and assert their independence in every maddening way they possibly can. Even if a teenage girl has a mom and a dad as blatantly awesome as Eric and Tami Taylor, she will still accuse them of being totally lame and attempt, as often as possible, to defy them.

Some of us have actually been teenage girls. And it was we, perhaps, who had the hardest time fully supporting Julie. Why? Because watching her every week was like looking in a mirror that reflected our own behavior back then. Those eye rolls. The back talk. That obstinate look that flashed across her face when she decided she was going out with Matt Saracen, damn it, whether her parents liked it or not. We recognized every expression and melodramatic hissy fit, and it made us resent her. Unlike Julie, we had reasons. Our parents were not as cool as the Taylors. They weren't even in the same galaxy of coolness. And if they had been, we never would have behaved the way Julie did.

Or so we tell ourselves. The truth is, teenage girl syndrome does funny things to a person. What we don't like to admit—and what Julie Taylor often forced us to recall—is that we were awfully bitchy to our mothers and fathers when we were sixteen, during moments when they were just trying to be good parents and didn't deserve to take so much crap from a kid who barely knew how to parallel park, let alone run her own life.

But the funny thing about teenagers is that, at times, you can see an adult start to peek through the storm clouds. So it was with Julie. She had plenty of moments where she stepped up, too: taking care of Gracie Belle in the mornings before school, ultimately supporting boyfriend Matt Saracen's decision to leave Dillon, and letting her mom and dad know how much she truly loved them, despite that constant tug-of-war between parents and child.

So maybe we love Julie Taylor precisely because she was a teenage girl, one who stayed out too late without calling, appealed to her dad when mom said no, insisted she deserved her own car, and fell in love deeply and fully in the way that only someone with a young, unfettered heart can. We loved her because, even though it sometimes made us squirm, she reminded us of ourselves at her age—and because, in the midst of all that, she made us see that a smart young woman just might emerge from that often self-involved, adolescent cocoon.

We love Julie Taylor because, as nearly every item on this list suggests, she always—refreshingly, hilariously, annoyingly—acted her age.

- Like all teens, Julie read great literature and concluded that it was actually describing a situation from her personal life—hence young Taylor's conclusion that *Moby Dick* was really the perfect metaphor for both the town of Dillon and the Dillon Panthers. "The magical white whale is the Holy Grail—the state championship," she explained. "The boat—I mean, the whalers are the team, right? The players and the coaches. Smash Williams is Queequeg, the hulking African zulu harpoon-hurling whale killer." Um, okay . . .

- When it appeared that Julie might have to spend an evening alone in the house with temporary Taylor border Buddy Garrity, she responded with her signature sense of perspective: "Are you even comprehending the depths of awkwardness? Why don't I just stick pins in my eyes?"

- Even though she didn't want to play in the powder-puff football game, she still pitched a fit when Matt, the team captain, didn't choose her until his third pick. (To be fair, given her quarterbacking skills, she kind of did deserve to go in the first round.)

- Like all young women, Julie knew how to work the system so she could go out and do what she wanted without her parents knowing. And by "work the system," what we mean is that she used her poor, nondescript friend Lois as a perpetual alibi.

- When Julie first decided she was ready to have sex with Matt, it was partly because she cared for him. But it was also because of science. "It's just the perfect opportunity for me to control the whole experience," she told Tyra Collette. "You know, get the information and gather the data."

- When Julie spoke openly with her dad about her desire to stay in Dillon at the end of season one, she began the conversation using classic teen speak: "My opinion is that when you first told me we were going to move to Dillon, I seriously wanted to vomit."

- After telling Matt that her dad had accepted that coaching job at TMU, something she knew she shouldn't have done, Julie once again resorted to a familiar teenage refrain to defend herself: "It's not my problem!"

- When Tami tried to be the caring, connected mother by asking Julie about her breakup with Matt, Julie cut off the conversation with a curt chilliness that only a sixteen-year-old girl is capable of. "Your baby's crying," she told her mom as Gracie Belle wailed in the next room. Cold. Blooded.

- Julie had a habit of developing crushes on older guys—the Swede, who looked more like Adrian Grenier than a Swedish guy; Noah Barnett, the English teacher who looked like Justin Timberlake; Ryan Lowry, the vaguely crunchy Habitat for Humanity team leader who looked like a J. Crew model; and, of course, Derek Bishop, the idiot college T.A. who looked like Peter Sarsgaard crossed with Topher Grace. Yet somehow, she managed to refrain from ever having the hots for Tim Riggins. This defied logic, but was also kind of impressive.

- The eldest Taylor daughter used her hard-earned Applebee's money to rebel by getting a tattoo on her ankle. This being Julie—the chick with indie-rock taste who still liked to dress up in flirty skirts and high heels—said tattoo was actually a girly little heart that looked more like an accidental magic marker stain than legitimate ink.

- After Eric caught Julie and Matt in bed together, postcoitus, Tami asked Julie what she had to say about it. She summed up the situation quite concisely: "He should have knocked."
- Even if Julie sometimes got on your nerves, there is no way your heart didn't rip open a little when she broke down sobbing while answering a question during the Academic Smackdown following Matt's sudden departure from Texas. What are the titles of the first and last novels by Thomas Wolfe? *Look Homeward, Angel* and *You Can't Go Home Again*. Oh, man. Brutal.
- After having an affair with Derek Bishop, her sleazeball, wussy, married college T.A., and getting slapped across the face and publicly humiliated by Derek's wife in the school library ("Julie Taylor is a slut!"), Julie responded naturally and appropriately: by going home to Dillon, then crashing her Chevy Aveo into a stone mailbox so she wouldn't have to go back to school.

When Julie first started having trouble with Matt Saracen, she confessed to her father that, "I see him turning into you, and me turning into my mom, and that just terrifies the crap out of me."

She was sixteen then, and had her world knocked upside down by the Swede, her father's part-time departure to TMU, and the arrival of her baby sister. By the time *Friday Night Lights* came to a close, she was eighteen and recovering from yet another shift in her earth's rotation brought on by life at college and Derek Bishop, aforementioned idiot T.A. But one thing had changed: the idea of her and Matt turning into her parents no longer frightened her.

Which is why, in the final episode, she joyfully accepted Matt's marriage proposal. And weirdly, this decision did not make Julie seem like an impetuous kid. It made her seem like a mature adult.

"You guys were married when you were our age," she told her parents during a contentious postengagement dinner. "How many different jobs have you had? How many times have you moved? And how many difficult things have you gone through? And you guys have made it work so well. You guys are my inspiration."

Julie Taylor could finally look at her mom and dad and see that if she and Matt did turn into them, they'd be pretty blessed.

With that realization, Julie and Matt appeared poised to embark on a beautiful, lifelong partnership. And little Julie Taylor—the girl who perpetually slammed the bedroom door when she didn't get her way, who turned eye-rolling into an art form, who often showed blatant disregard for her parents' wishes—finally grew up.

We felt we really had to always stay with the basic premise of the show, which was to try to make it as authentic and real and honest as possible.

—**Jason Katims**, interviewed by Alan Sepinwall,
"Interview: 'Friday Night Lights' showrunner
Jason Katims post-mortems the series finale,"
What's Alan Watching on HitFix.com

The Best Reality Show on Television

ARIELLA PAPA

When *Friday Night Lights* hit the scene in 2006, my day job was watching reality television shows and then creating promos for the networks. I am not the biggest reality-TV fan. The shows seemed completely inhuman, and the stars were anything but real. It was all so contrived. But given the percentage of television occupied by reality shows, especially back then, they were impossible to avoid. I found myself spending my nonwork hours craving an escape from "reality"—which was when I found *Friday Night Lights.*

While the reality-TV people I was watching for work seemed maniacally constructed and controlled by the production equivalent of Dr. Frankenstein's lab, *Friday Night Lights*—a fictional show, written by professional writers and acted by professional actors—felt totally authentic and true to life. The characters seemed more like people than the *actual* people in reality shows. Landry Clarke, Matt Saracen, Smash Williams, Tyra Collette, Lyla Garrity, and Jason Street became as real to me as many people I know. Somehow I found myself actually caring about their lives. I wondered what was going on in the Taylor household between episodes. I worried—really worried—about the Riggins brothers and their questionable decisions. (Copper wire? Stripping cars? Say it ain't so.) And now, with the show's end, I feel myself saddened by the loss of these people I have come to love. I'll miss them truly. And that is a testament to the creators behind the scenes, who skillfully produced a show that doesn't feel like it was produced at all.

It isn't an accident that Dillon and its inhabitants feel so alive. It took the hard work and smart choices of many supremely talented writers, directors, actors, and directions to make *Friday Night Lights* feel so authentic.

One of those choices had to do with setting. Part of why we feel like we really are in Dillon while watching *Friday Night Lights* is because the show really *was* filmed in Dillon—or, since there is no actual Dillon, as close to it as any place could be. The dry landscape, the burning sun, the shops, and other local color left no doubt that we were in Texas. "We can see America from here," said Michael Waxman, the in-house director and producer. "We don't have to work much on making it seem real."

But what *did* we know about Texas, from watching the first episode or any of the episodes that followed? Not much, really. Normally at the beginning of a show we are shown familiar locales to remind us where we are. Oh look, it's the Hollywood sign, or hey, here we are again at the Trump offices in New York City. This technique is supposed to draw us in to the familiar and make us feel like we know the characters better than we do. Dillon, Texas, isn't a part of most peoples' frames of reference. And yet still it feels natural and believable in a way those staged building shots don't.

Rather than using a set or some back lot made to look like a town, *Friday Night Lights* was shot on location in Austin and its environs. And because, as the show's head writer and executive producer, Jason Katims, told Maureen Ryan in a 2007 interview:

> Because we haven't built a single set, and everything is in a real place, we as writers are put in a position where we're very free to explore. We can go into Tyra's house as soon as we can go into the coach's house, or Saracen's house, or Landry's house for that matter. What's different about that, as opposed to how most TV productions are set up, is that for the most part you build sets, which means you're in that one place.

Often sets don't have four walls, much less multiple rooms with real scenery through the windows.

All this made Dillon believable in a way that, say, a castle on a mountain where one man will choose the love of his life from a collection of beautiful hopefuls could never be.

Location isn't the only step toward authenticity that *Friday Night Lights* took. Another major part of the show, the football scenes, seemed real for a simple reason: they were. The games may have been a little less than accurate, but when we watched the Dillon Panthers play we were often watching a real live football team, the Pflugerville Panthers, in their stadium, with their cheerleaders, in their uniforms, in their team colors. They served as the Dillon Panthers' stand-ins.

None of the show's main actors are actual West Texans, but local people also made their way into the show as extras, often performing their actual professions: the owner of the store in season one where Matt bought Julie Taylor those apology earrings, for example. A real-life preacher was called to give a church sermon. The show even had cameos from Texas football coaches Mike Leach and Mack Brown. All of these extras playing "real-life" parts helped blur the line between reality and fiction.

Certain storytelling choices did the same. The pilot started with a cold open, which means the show cuts right into the story from the very beginning, straight from commercial. There was no happy theme song preparing us for a story. From the opening words in the pilot—"Good morning, West Texas"—we were immediately there in West Texas, in Dillon. We got thrust right into the action in a way that felt like Dillon had always been there—living, breathing, organic—and we were just realizing its existence.

We met the characters in similarly quick glances: the coach being discussed on the very radio he was listening to on his way to the Panthers' den; Matt with his grandma, then getting picked up by his buddy Landry; Tim Riggins sleeping off the drink. There wasn't the usual exposition that happens in a pilot. We didn't get dialogue for the sole purpose of revealing backstory. There was no "new guy in town" to follow as he and we got acquainted with new places and new people. From the beginning it seemed as though we were just jumping into conversations that were going on whether or not there was an audience (which early on . . . there wasn't). We entered Dillon as we would have a real town: joining lives and stories already in progress.

These characters were (for the most part) also placed in realistic situations. In reality TV the situations are contrived to the point of bombast, and the characters are called upon to participate in increasingly preposterous scenarios. But on *Friday Night Lights* there was rarely a situation that didn't seem plausible to the characters or relatable to the viewers (with the notable exception of the season two murder gimmick—generally considered to be a desperate attempt at gaining viewers with a situation that was more like the sorts of things going on elsewhere on television).

Friday Night Lights' characters felt alive. What appeared at first glance to be one-dimensional archetypes—the cheerleader, the nerd, the bad boy—were allowed greater complexity right off the bat (a stark contrast to reality shows, where real, presumably complex people are reduced to one-dimensional archetypes).

The filming choices allowed these characters to behave like real people, too. When filming, often the first take, the most organic one, was the one that wound up being beamed to us on our couches at home. In real life, you say things, and that's it. There's no redo. No matter who may have been hurt or what chain of events your words may have put into motion, they can't be unsaid. The characters on *Friday Night Lights* interacted accordingly. During science teacher Glenn Reed's confession to Coach Taylor about kissing Tami, we giggled and cringed, wishing he could have a do-over. (Conversely, when watching shows like *The Hills* you can't help but think that you might be watching the umpteenth take of a certain situation. You'll often hear lines delivered *so* unnaturally you can almost hear the off-camera producer prodding these people with dialogue.)

Friday Night Lights' characters weren't really played so much as inhabited. Peter Berg, the creator of the show, is an actor himself. He works "loose," as he said in an interview with About. com, giving his actors a certain amount of control over their characters. He famously told them that no matter what instruction they received from the show directors they—the actors—were the experts on their characters. Actors were given the specs for a scene and told what needed to be accomplished. Loose dialogue was provided, but it was the actors—the character experts—who decided how to get where they needed to go.

Everyone has a different story about what exactly Berg said in his initial pep talk, but the message was clear—the people who worked on the show had the freedom to do what they needed to make the show and its characters more real. That's a lot of freedom for anyone to have in television, where so much is determined by network executives trying to anticipate focus groups, advertisers, and the never-silent online critic.

The show also chose to use stand-ins only rarely. In most of these productions, actors don't act with each other. There is no need for everyone to be on set for other people's close-ups. The first time I saw a film being produced firsthand, this knowledge changed the way I watched movies and television forever. I had seen behind the curtain. Some of the magic was gone. From then on, whenever I watched movies or television, I realized that the actor I was watching give a heartfelt speech to his costar was most likely acting against the costar's body double. On *Friday Night Lights*, the actors worked together all the time. This not only added to the speed and efficiency of shoot time; it made the rapport between actors that much stronger and more genuine. Each take is enhanced by a fellow actor's reaction instead of a stand-in's.

This policy also meant the show's actors could develop personal relationships with each other, a phenomenon that is certainly not unheard of but that is surprisingly uncommon in TV and movies. Kyle Chandler and Connie Britton, who play Coach Eric and Tami Taylor, met every morning they were shooting together to have coffee and flesh out what their characters would say and how they would say it. Those conversations resulted in some of the best moments in the show. In the final season they scratched what was meant to be an all-out fight scene and opted to merely have Tami say, "Eighteen years." In real life, dramatic moments rarely happen in long speeches; they happen in quick phrases like "eighteen years" and in the glances and pauses between them.

Perhaps it was Chandler and Britton's close friendship that led to their familiarity never feeling forced. We recognize what it looks like when two people know each other well and care about each other. And Chandler and Britton made the often falsely passionate or faking bachelors or bachelorettes who expect to find their true love on a reality set seem all the more laughable. Eric and Tami's love felt real.

The quiet moments in *Friday Night Lights* frequently felt like the most authentic parts of the show. As actress Aimee Teegarden said in a recent *LA Times* article, "The most poignant moments on that show were when there was no dialogue. A lot happened in those quiet moments." Think of the scene that took place at Sunday Mass the morning after Teegarden's character, Julie, and Matt did the controversial "it" for the first time. The characters exchanged glances, smiling, completely effervescent in the throes not of underage lust gone unchecked, but the magic of real adolescent love. With nothing but facial expressions they told the story of two people who had taken an enormous step in their lives and had no regret about who they chose to take it with. In this scene, there was also no doubt that both Teegarden and Zach Gilford, the actor who played Matt, were present, and that the two knew each other well. It's hard to fake that kind of chemistry acting against a stand-in. It's a kind of magic that has to happen in the moment.

In *Entertainment Weekly, Friday Night Lights'* executive producer Jeffrey Reiner described the show's documentary-style shooting method this way: "no rehearsal, no blocking, just three cameras and we shoot." This is similar to what you'd expect from reality TV—the goal is, after all, supposed to be to capture reality as it happens. Except that *Friday Night Lights'* three-camera orchestration felt far more seamless than reality shows' sweeping helicopter shots and tiny cameras mounted on dashboards. Those methods, even used to shoot so-called "real" events, feel invasive and far stagier than a show that is 100 percent staged.

The term "fly on the wall" is used to describe the type of documentary film style where the camera documents the action without interfering. But while *Friday Night Lights'* filming style is nonobtrusive, that doesn't mean that the cameras just observed from afar; they were often smack dab in the middle of everything. In the pilot, during the scene at the car dealership before the first game, we moved through multiple conversations, pushing in on reactions, returning to see the unexpected ends to situations we'd seen snippets of earlier. The creators didn't need to set up the scene—we were made to feel like we were right there in the middle of it all, a fellow party guest. This fly didn't stay on the wall; it landed on people's noses. In fact, we rarely saw wide shots (the opposite of a close-up) during dialogue throughout the series—something most shows use frequently to set the scene.

The directors and producers of *Friday Night Lights* saw the filming and the editing as an extension of the storytelling. Jason Katims felt that editing "is writing. So in the editing rooms, you're dealing with a lot of raw footage, scenes are being assembled and put together and rebuilt." The show's editors were given the freedom to make sure all of the footage was put together in a way that enhanced the filming techniques. In the pilot, going back and forth between those reaction shots during the first game and the hospital where Jason Street was being examined was mind blowing. The cuts were all fast and furious, but we bought it as viewers because it never distracted from the show.

The reality show equivalent to the climactic pigskin throw-down on *Friday Night Lights* are those laborious elimination scenes where someone is being given their walking papers. These scenes are edited to the point of claustrophobia, lingering on a face or cutting to contestants for a far longer period of time than it would really take for a guy to give a girl a flower or award someone a winner. It's how they make drama out of contrived situations, and it's hard to miss. It just plain feels unnatural. But on *Friday Night Lights* the editing remained unnoticed, no matter how stylized it became.

How could such stylized editing go by unnoticed? Because going unnoticed is the definition of good editing. If a viewer comments on the editing of the show, it means they have just been taken out of the story—they are aware that they're watching fiction.

Music should work the same way. On many shows (and, yes, especially reality shows) music is used as shorthand for emotions. *Psycho-* or *Jaws*-like music lets us know who the "villain" is. Clown or slapstick music attempts to highlight the humor in a scene that just isn't that funny.

On the other hand, in *Friday Night Lights* the songs seemed to live with and heighten the scenes' natural moods instead of desperately trying to create some vague sense of drama that isn't even really there. Music was layered into the show so well—whether it was the familiar notes of "Explosions in the Sky" or the latest hit by The Hold Steady—that it was as overlooked but as crucial as the sound of a football hitting an open receiver's hands. Songs emphasized the naturally occurring energy in scenes, heightening their emotional impact.

I was regularly moved to tears or chills by this show, and by these characters, who I wanted to know more and felt I understood better with every hour I spent in their company. Working in the industry, I realized all the pieces and people that had to work together so seamlessly to create this one amazing whole. And I was in awe.

Now the show is over. And it's not the kind of reality show where I can anticipate a reunion episode to let me know how it all turns out for the town. Although it's difficult to imagine I'll never see these people again, I just have to let them go.

When Tyra wrote her letter to college back in season three, I watched that scene again and again. Her words resonated with me: "I want to be important. I want to be the best person I can be. I want to define myself instead of having others define me" ("Underdogs," 3-12). And now that Tyra's off my screen for good, it really seems possible that she is off somewhere having the "interesting and surprising life" she wrote about in her college essay.

I choose to believe that about all the characters. I choose to believe that they have gone on to be who they wanted to be, to define themselves instead of being defined by any producer, network executive, or viewer. Sure, I won't know for certain how it ends for every single person I have followed so carefully for the past five years. But in real life, you never do.

There's a level of honest, raw humanity in *Friday Night Lights* that few TV dramas have ever achieved. Over and over and over, the show and its characters wore their hearts on their sleeves, in a way that somehow made them more solid than characters on other series of comparable quality.

That rawness made the show great, but it was also likely one of the aspects (along with the high school football setting) that kept the show from being a hit, as most viewers don't turn to TV to be confronted by emotions as powerful as the ones this series brought up. Watching *Friday Night Lights* often felt like being put through a ringer. You felt like part of the town, and the team, and you bled with the characters and cried with them, and on occasion you got to soar with them, too.

—**Alan Sepinwall**, "Review: 'Friday Night Lights':
A look back at its greatness and its greatest moments,"
What Alan's Watching on HitFix.

WHY WE LOVE

. . . Tyra Collette

To rely on T&A, or not to rely on T&A?

For Tyra Collette, that was perpetually the question.

Here was a supposed high schooler who looked like she had just stepped out of the pages of *Playboy*, all blonde hair, killer bod, and wicked eyes. She was a Collette, with a MILF for a mom and a sister who stripped for tips at the premier Dillon nudie bar. Looking like that, with that kind of pedigree, she could easily have continued breaking hearts and serving up sizzlin' steak fajitas at Applebee's for as long as her heart desired.

But Tyra Collette's heart and, more importantly, her mind wanted more.

She wanted to go to college. She wanted to, in her words, break the Collette mold. She wanted to be seen as a woman who had more to offer than one-night stands and saucy repartee.

Because she desired all of those things so desperately and also happened to have a Texas-sized chip on her shoulder, Tyra could be more than a little nasty. This girl put both the spit *and* the fire into spitfire.

She was often less than kind to Lyla Garrity. ("Hey, cheatin' cheerleader bitch," she once called to Lyla when she was stranded on the side of a road. "Want a ride?") And she had a bad habit of callously using and abusing Landry Clarke; does anyone else still twitch with horror when they remember the time she coldly told him: "Look in a mirror. I don't know what I was thinking with you." She didn't really mean it, but still—cuts like a freakin' knife, Tyra.

That said, over time and with some crucial assistance from Landry and Tami Taylor, Tyra Collette matured. She had always been the kind of girl who was willing to go after her mother's abusive boyfriend with a hot poker. But she turned into one who insisted on changing a damn tire herself to prove she didn't need a man, who could walk away from a cowboy named Cash, and who ultimately proved she could get accepted at UT, despite the naysayers— including herself—who thought that acceptance letter would never come. She ultimately revealed to the world that Tyra Collette was someone to respect and admire, not just to ogle.

For that—and for the reasons noted below—we love Tyra Collette.

- When a random Dillon girl openly wept over Jason Street's injury at the Alamo Freeze, it was Tyra who knocked her out of her sobbing stupor: "You don't even know Jason Street, so stop crying. Okay, no, seriously? Stop."

- Important fact about life: when playing in a powder-puff football game, stay the hell out of Tyra Collette's way. Because it doesn't matter if you're playing flag and not tackle: Tyra will take you down.

- Only Tyra would refer to the Landing Strip as the "Women with Low Self-Esteem Palace."

- When an older, handsome guy with an interesting job— say, an investment banker or a rodeo cowboy—showed up in town, Tyra was guaranteed to capture his attention. Any relationship with said gentlemen was also guaranteed not to end well and, most likely, to involve Tyra winding up alone and depressed at a hotel.

- Tyra could pull off a variety of hair styles: long and flowing, blunt bob, even straight and super-dark. The only one she couldn't rock was the perm. The perm was just bad.
- That girl could spike the hell out of a volleyball—especially when she aimed it at the head of Tim Riggins.
- Tyra Collette knew politics, which is why she got elected student council president based on her unbeatable "I'll Throw a Prom Where Everyone Gets Laid" platform.
- When Landry finally called Tyra on her use-and-abuse-him nonsense, she not only owned up to it, she arranged for the most prime Crucifictorious gig ever.
- After being convinced she could not write a decent college essay, she crafted one that wound up becoming one of the most tear-jerking moments ever on the show. "I want to grow up and be generous and big hearted, the way people have been with me," she wrote. "I want an interesting and surprising life. It's not that I think I'm going to get all these things, I just want the possibility of getting them. College represents possibility. The possibility that things are going to change. I can't wait."

When Tyra briefly made an appearance in season five, she showed up just long enough to wake Tim out of his postprison stupor and let him know that she planned to go into politics. ("Like Sarah Palin?" Tim asked. "No, you ass," she responded. "Out of all the people, really?")

As Tim and Tyra shared a beer, he suggested that maybe the two of them could get back together someday, perhaps even find a way to pursue their dreams together. And for once, the idea of Tim and Tyra in a relationship seemed potentially healthy and right. That's because we were looking at Tyra 2.0: an independent woman with her own dreams, but one at least willing to consider a merger.

WHY WE LOVE . . . Character Series from the *Washington Post*'s Jen Chaney

WHY WE LOVE
. . . Brian "Smash" Williams

urn on ESPN right now. There's a good chance that at this moment or a moment in the very near future, you'll see a football player who looks and sounds a lot like Smash Williams.

Supremely talented. Completely charismatic. And yes, cocky as all hell, the sort of guy who thinks the game was never played properly until someone first put the ball in his hands and let him run it in for a TD.

Smash was definitely that stereotypical athlete, but one whose arrogance was outweighed by his affability. He had a baby face to go with that swagger, and a vulnerability that made it impossible to pigeonhole him as just another conceited jerk.

As gifted as he was, the path from Dillon Panther to eventual Texas A&M Aggie was not a smooth and easy one for Smash Williams. Smash's rising star was brought low multiple times, first by the revelation of his steroid use, then by the loss of his scholarship to TMU and a devastating knee injury. As an African American, he also frequently faced racism and the internal conflict that came with it: speak out against bigotry, or focus on silently rising above it? Over the course of the show, Smash did both. Not surprisingly, neither option made the racism go away.

Even if Smash didn't single-handedly eradicate prejudice in Dillon, Texas (shocker), he did achieve something pretty spectacular: he managed to turn from a cocky high school running back into a grateful, hardworking, and, okay, probably sometimes still cocky, college football sensation.

We also love Smash Williams because:

- While rapping during a party at Garrity Motors, he promised that the Panthers would get diabolical, like "Tom Cruise gets scientological."
- He frequently referred to himself in the third person, as if he were both the protagonist in an epic story and the omniscient narrator who already knew how well it would turn out.
- Thanks to his insightful literary analysis—"Ulysses is a pimp"—we will never read *The Odyssey* the same way again.
- Smash was the kind of guy who would take a break at the Alamo Freeze to give Matt Saracen sex advice, advice that involved football analogies ("You still gotta read the coverage"), while not condoning premarital relations ("I ain't tryin' to encourage sex out of wedlock. Don't put it on ol' Smash"), and the importance of logistics (such as securing a cabin-turned-almost-love-shack for doing the deed).
- Smash had a special gift for giving pithy nicknames to people he disliked. Hence his reference to Voodoo Tatum as "Doodoo" and his rude but admittedly funny use of "Chip and Dale" to greet a very white Laribee player with sizable teeth.
- When Mac McGill made racist remarks about some of the black players on the Dillon Panthers squad, Smash was proud enough to note the inappropriateness of those comments and forgiving enough to eventually give Mac the benefit of the doubt (although, frankly, it would have made more sense if Smash stayed pissed at him for the rest of his career).
- Smash made what was, without question, the best joke at the Dillon Panther roast: "For as long as I've known Tim

Riggins, there's only two phrases that can put a smile on his face. No. 1: We're going to state. And No. 2: The results are in. You are not the father."

- The ladies' man was smart enough to know that amidst all the Waverlys, Noelles, and other females in his orbit, there was one woman he could truly count on to love him: his feisty, whip-smart, wonderful momma.

- When he could no longer play for the Panthers because of his suspension, Smash still found the backbone to show up in the locker room and pump up his team, right before he (God bless that poor kid) broke down sobbing because he couldn't join them on the field.

- While TMU revoked Smash's scholarship because they thought his "character was questionable" due to an altercation at a movie theater, we knew his character was anything but. And there was no question that the kid at the multiplex deserved some sort of comeuppance for being a racist, sexist, disrespectful fool.

When Smash got the phone call telling him he finally got a spot at Texas A&M after a walk-on tryout, we were just as teary and joyful as the football star himself.

Sadly, we never got to see more of Smash after *Friday Night Lights'* third season. He was shown at a distance on a TV screen a couple of times, though—an Aggie running the ball up the field. It appeared Smash Williams finally was getting closer to what he wanted: a promising career as a star running back.

We can only assume those endorsement deals he bragged that he would eventually snag—"I'm going to do Big Macs and Whoppers. Coke and Pepsi. Look, I'm gonna bring the whole world together, baby"—will be coming his way any day now.

Friday Night Lights emitted a feeling of expansiveness. The expansiveness of the flat Texas land and the big Texas sky, passing by as if viewed from the rolled-down window of a pickup truck. The expansiveness of the crowds gathered in the stands each Friday night, illuminated by tall stadium lights.

Even the soundtrack, from the highly emotive Texas-based band Explosions in the Sky, added to a sense of expanding space, a feeling that the universe will always be bigger than we can comprehend.

But the series showed that we decide how to fill that space, and what we send out into it, like the prayer Coach Taylor sends out in episode one:

> *Give all of us gathered here tonight the strength to remember that life is so very fragile.*
>
> *We are all vulnerable, and we will all, at some point in our lives, fall.*
>
> *We will all fall.*
>
> *We must carry this in our hearts—that what we have is special. That it can be taken from us, and that when it is taken from us, we will be tested.*
>
> *We will be tested to our very souls.*
>
> *We will now all be tested.*
>
> *It is these times, it is this pain, that allows us to look inside ourselves.*

Amen.

—**Dyana Herron**, "So Long, Friday Night Lights,"
ImageJournal.org

WHY WE LOVE
. . . Buddy Garrity

Buddy Garrity is a simple Texas man. He loves his red meat. He loves his three kids, even when two of them clearly appeared to be turning into hippies after moving to California with their mother. And he loves, looo-oooves his football. (That's foot-bawl, by the way. It's impossible to speak of Buddy without sliding some twang into one's speech.)

Admittedly, Buddy is not the easiest guy to like. He's loud. He's a heavy breather. He's very pushy, especially when it comes to providing recruiting assistance to Coach Eric Taylor, or demanding the installation of Jumbotrons, or insisting on bringing a deep-fried turkey to the Taylors' Thanksgiving dinner. In his own words, he's a sinner—the kind of guy who cheats on his wife, occasionally falls in the mud after drinking too much, and installs a mailbox where it really, really doesn't belong.

Despite all of this, we love Buddy Garrity, because at his big ol' buttinsky core, he's got a heart made out of gold—the same gold, presumably, one would find on his Dillon Panther championship ring. Sure, Buddy throws around his cash to get what he wants and inappropriately exerts his influence, not unlike a certain smug a-hole by the name of Joe McCoy. But unlike McCoy, Buddy is capable of compassion and decency. He's a teddy bear . . . granted, a teddy bear who gets into fights at strip clubs and winds up getting arrested for drunken disorderliness. But still, a teddy bear all the same.

Buddy Garrity's eyes weren't always clear. But his heart was always impossibly full. And for that, as well as the reasons noted below, we love Buddy Garrity.

- He used the slogan "I'm Your Buddy" in commercials for Garrity Motors, with zero sense of irony.
- When Buddy briefly shacked up with the Taylors, he made sure to stay out of their way. It was no inconvenience at all, for example, when he forced Tami to make pork chops or used some notepad detective work to figure out Eric was having dinner with someone from TMU. ("That's a little something I learned on *Magnum, P.I.* Works pretty dadgum well, too.")
- After repeatedly cheating on his wife and getting slapped by his latest mistress in front of half the community following Sunday services—in front of a church! Seriously, Buddy!— Buddy still believed he could win his way back into his wife's heart simply by making a scrapbook.
- Buddy is a generous employer who hires just about anyone who needs some work: Santiago Herrera, Jason Street, Tim Riggins, Angela Collette, even Henry Saracen. He is also generous in his assessment of certain people's skills. "I just hired Matt Saracen's dad to be a salesman," Buddy told Tim, "and I don't mind telling you that that man could not sell a life preserver to a drowning man."
- Buddy once was, and probably still is, under the decidedly wrong impression that Jumbotron is two words.
- Only Buddy Garrity could demonstrate how much he cared about Santiago (seriously, whatever happened to that kid?) by taking his most prized possessions to the Taylors' house to keep them safe from Santiago's friends . . . then taking

them right back to his apartment and placing them on his mantle in ridiculously prominent spots. That's Buddy: one extreme or the blatantly obvious other.

- After blowing all of Lyla's college money on a misguided investment—in a strip mall, of all things—Buddy manned up enough to ask the dreaded Uncle Gary for some financial help. When it came to his children, at least, Buddy Garrity was willing to swallow his pride.

- If Buddy Garrity never did one single other admirable thing in his entire life, we'd love him for this alone: that brilliant "go to hell" speech he made at Joe McCoy's Dillon Panthers backyard party. "I'm not a Panther anymore . . . Joe, I tried, but ever since you got here you've been a cancer to me, you've been a cancer to my friends and you've been a cancer to this team. One more thing: Clear eyes, full hearts, can't lose." God bless you, Buddy Garrity.

- Did we mention how strongly and unwaveringly Buddy showed his affection for steak? Fine, let's let him say it for us: "Nature already has meat. It's called a cow."

- When it became apparent that the East Dillon Lions would no longer exist and would merge with the Dillon Panthers, Buddy knew he had to seize the opportunity to be the big booster-club man in Dillon again. Or, to put it another way, two words: superteam.

Buddy Garrity will never leave the Dillon Panther football field. Not mentally, certainly. And as it turns out, not physically either.

In the final moments of *Friday Night Lights*, we could see that Buddy was now happily motoring along the Dillon High sidelines, driving a golf cart once steered by the mighty but fallen Joe McCoy and Wade Aikman. And we noted that he was right there in the locker room, supervising the hanging of a sign that read: "Clear Eyes. Full Hearts. Can't Lose."

In the end, it was Buddy Garrity—occasional jackass and always loyal friend—who made sure that the Dillon Panthers would never, ever forget his friend Eric Taylor.

Pantherama!

The Psychology of Sports Fanaticism in *Friday Night Lights*

JEREMY CLYMAN

Perhaps the most striking quality of *Friday Night Lights* is the underlying theme of sports fanaticism. On the surface, *Friday Night Lights* is a show about a caring coach and his supportive family, the love of a game, and a group of high school athletes learning to become the best version of themselves. Underneath, however, sports fanaticism drives a far more dramatic and complex narrative in which high school football players contend with celebrity and crisis, a town's mood fluctuates with each passing game, and the well-being of the show's relatable protagonists— the Taylor family—is constantly threatened by the crazed Panther culture.

The pilot episode illustrated this darker undercurrent at work. Viewers were introduced to opening night of Dillon Panther football, in which overwhelming scrutiny transforms thoughtful and mild-mannered individuals like Coach Taylor and Brian "Smash" Williams into more frantic and fearful versions of themselves. We watched as the phrase "state championship" passed through the town's collective lips and induced a state of glazed tranquility, as if sports fanaticism were some cultish force that had brainwashed the town into believing that a state championship meant a better life for all. This unsettling sentiment picked up speed throughout the episode, culminating in images of pep rallies, pancake breakfasts, and—most unnerving of all—the town's youth gathering around star quarterback Jason Street like disciples around a religious deity.

But as the show continued to unfold and we learned more about the Dillon Panthers, the meaning of sports fanaticism evolved—and what had initially seemed like a force of psychological destruction turned into something much more complex and profound.

Panther players who had seemed so scarred and overwhelmed by sports fanaticism, over time, began to brim with health. For Smash Williams, his fragile and feverish pursuit of the limelight matured into a quiet grace and dignity that propelled him through racial tensions and knee injuries. Then there was the ex–star quarterback, Jason Street, who fell into a spiral of aimless despair as the town's cripple before ultimately wheeling himself out of Dillon and into a promising new life. Like a double-edge sword, the phenomenon of sports fandom seemed to suffocate the Panther players and its fans while also providing a healthy dose of growth and resiliency. Thus, while *Friday Night Lights* does plenty to acknowledge the dark side of sports fanaticism, the ultimate message seems to match what psychologists are now demonstrating—fandom is much more than what it seems.

The Real-World Fan

In modern society, it's normal for people to pay for tickets, sit in stands, and watch two teams of children compete with another. But as the pilot episode's portrait of the Dillon community suggested, our perception of this seemingly simple and innocent activity is complicated by centuries of human evolution.

Evolutionary psychologists often remind us that we have evolved from more primitive times when small tribes warred with each other and life and death hung in the balance. Many psychologists have speculated that sports have replaced the function of tribal warfare in modern communities—especially in light of the fact that religion, the extended family structure, and other traditional social structures have fallen out of favor. On some subtle, subconscious level, therefore, we may perceive athletes not as ordinary people but as warriors. And we may perceive sports not as some light diversion but as a timeless ritual of critical importance to our sense of self. Sporting events like football may induce such a perceptual shift not just because associations to a more primitive world are triggered, but because the core psychological needs that evolved within our ancestors, the ones that led them to engage in war, continue to operate within us to this day.

Our brains are designed to join packs, and a sports team is one of the few packs in modern society open to new members. Once we join a pack, we instinctively seek out ways to strengthen our bond, whether by aggrandizing the group to which we belong or demeaning rival groups. This primitive urge to promote the "in-group" and attack the "out-group" leads to an array of cognitive distortions. This was first captured in a now-infamous study on group bias. In the late sixties, an Iowa grade school teacher decided to conduct an experiment by dividing her third-grade class into groups based on eye color. Within minutes after pitting the "blue-eyed" group against the "brown-eyed" group, a funny thing happened—sweet seven-year-olds became sadists who insulted and shunned each other based purely on this newly established group membership and status. Such a finding parallels the ways in which the Dillon community often treated rival teams and, at times, its own players—but why does this happen?

A significant portion of the answer has to do with self-esteem and the process of identification. As fans we feel truly represented by our teams. And research confirms that something as simple as the outcome of a game affects our psyche in ways that are much more profound than might be expected. For instance, directly after our team wins, we are more optimistic in predicting our performance on various tasks—from a romantic date to mental activities like word games. How we view ourselves seems to be inextricably tied to how our team performs. Fittingly, this powerful emotional investment is reflected in our physiology, as we experience the same hormonal surges and other physiological changes during a game as the players do. In fact, images of our favorite sports team have been found to produce the same degree of heart rate and perspiration activity as images of eroticism or animal fights.

And because our identity and our sports teams tend to fuse together, thereby ratcheting up the emotional stakes, our psyches rush to our aid in an effort to maintain a sense of stability and esteem. Understanding the ways in which we unintentionally play with reality when it comes to the perceptions of our teams (in-group) and its rivals (out-group) is the focus of a second line of research. This literature has shown, for instance, that in response to defeat we tend to blame the team's failure on officiating, bad luck, or other external excuses, thus avoiding the more depressing conclusion that something intrinsic or unchangeable about our team, such as talent, is at fault. We tend to evaluate our team and its players more favorably than rival teams, and we harbor memories and expectations of our sports team that are more positive than the facts would suggest. We claim credit for our team's success (i.e., saying "we won"), but switch to a more detached perspective in response to defeat (i.e., saying "they lost" instead of "we lost")—cognitive proclivities termed *basking in reflected glory* and *cutting off reflected failure*, respectively. Similarly, we are much more likely to wear our sports attire after a win than after a defeat. And perhaps most adaptively, we automatically and constantly recalibrate our perceptions of our team's likelihood of success—we become most pessimistic about our team's chances right before kickoff, and when the clock expires, finalizing a defeat, we are already cushioning the pain of failure by concluding that our team's chances were never really as good as we'd thought.

In short, we perceive the story of our sports team through rose-colored glasses. What this list of self-deceiving, perceptual hiccups suggests is that we misperceive information, but in consistent, calculated ways that help us adapt to pain.

Sports Fanaticism as Pathology

The portrait of a sports fanatic was not always viewed in such a scientific, nuanced manner, however. Before we learned that group processes distort the perspectives of the healthy and unhealthy alike, early psychological literature attacked fandom as a force of pathology. In an essay entitled "Fandom as Pathology: The Consequences of Characterization," by media scholar Joli Jensen, fans were thought of either as obsessive loners lost in fantasy and suffering from isolation or as members of a frenzied crowd prone to contagion and violence. Further, the relationship between a fan and his or her team was understood as a psychological act of inadequacy and compensation. Boisterous cheering was seen as the desperate squeals of the socially crippled as they made their last, ultimately inadequate stand for human connection. Research flowed from this model for over a decade, linking "sports fan" to such negative descriptors as "irrational," "lazy," "alienated," "aggressive," "alcoholic," and "easily swayed losers." In turn, journal articles like "Sports is the New Opium of the People" expressed fears that sports could become "a mania, a drug far more potent and widespread than any mere chemical substance" capable of disrupting life on a societal level.

Though rational empirical study has found little data to support this model, the motif of fandom run amok continues to thrive in many modern-day narratives. *Friday Night Lights* joins a long list that includes such recent films as *Varsity Blues*, in which teenage athletes struggle to cope with extraordinary pressure, and *Big Fan*, where an obsessive fan slowly decompensates. There is a very primitive, almost villainous character lurking in the subtextual depths of the show known simply as "the town." This figure embodies the thousands of Dillon citizens who are, in different ways and to varying degrees, emotionally invested in the Panthers.

The psyche of "the town" surfaced through a variety of voices. First, there was Slammin' Sammy talk radio. Here, "the town" emerged as a source of critical insatiability. After every Friday-night game the radio waves were jammed with fans calling in to second-guess Coach Taylor. They described every conceivable imperfection with the team's most recent performance. Every sideline decision, every on-field play was examined and then re-examined. Why did Coach Taylor run the ball so much? If he had let Matt Saracen go deep then that fourth-quarter fumble never would have happened, and we'd be rejoicing in victory right now, instead of oozing with despair! Such ruminative cycles churned until midweek when, like a predator devouring its prey, "the town" decided it had thoroughly digested last week's game and reset its sights on the upcoming game. At this time an equally dysfunctional discussion began, marked by insecurities, speculative drivel, and predictions of nightmare scenarios.

We also came to know "the town" through Coach Taylor's eyes. Early in season one, Coach Taylor warned his players that "the town" harbored sky-high expectations and could grow quite restless and uneasy in response to loss. When the Panthers lost their second game of the season because Matt failed to adequately fill the shoes of the paralyzed Jason Street, chaos ensued. The following week saw Coach Taylor cornered by angry fans, his job threatened. In fact, many of the early episodes depicted a dejected Coach Taylor, head in hands, wondering how his family was going to survive his seemingly inevitable firing. Further, the Panther players were harassed. Matt was forced to clean spray paint off his personalized Panther billboard—just one of many acts of vandalism that were perpetrated as the Panther faithful drowned their sorrows in alcohol.

Lastly, "the town" surfaced through the actions of its most significant and vocal members—namely, Buddy Garrity, head of the all-powerful Panther booster club, and Mayor Rodell, head of the town. They wielded their almost monarchical powers in the service of a Panther state championship. Early in season three, for instance, the energetic and capable Tami Taylor, newly promoted from guidance counselor to principal, discovered that the high school's academic performance and classroom resources were collapsing while the football program continued to thrive. She rerouted significant funds, prioritizing the student body over the Panther program in a move that generated an almost comical storm of protest and pressure: Tami's job was threatened and the rerouted funds were frozen. In one scene, exhausted and defeated, Tami met with Coach Taylor at Applebee's for their weekly dinner date and proclaimed, "What is wrong with these people?" She had a look on her face that said, "I am a rational human being. And although I've always been one to admire small-town mystique, I can't stand the craziness of Dillon anymore. This is worse than the Twilight Zone."

Although Coach Taylor sympathized and largely concurred with his victimized wife, he reminded her that "the town" had acted in a predictable fashion. He flashed one of those grimaces that was part amusement, part exacerbation, and seemed to say, "Yes, you made your principled stand loud and clear. And although it's quite principled, Dillon does not want to hear it. Dillon cares about football more than education, it cares about the short-term success of its team more than the long-term success of its citizens—and that's the harsh reality."

It indeed seems as though "the town," intentionally or not, exhibits every symptom of the fan-as-pathology model. This point was punctuated midway through season one when the show finally put a face to the subtextual character. It was a random and rainy weekday, and Coach Taylor had just ducked into the Alamo Freeze with his daughter, Julie, to order some take-out. Within minutes, Julie was cornered by an embittered Panther fan who menacingly inquired, "Has your dad started packing yet? Things can get real ugly around here when you lose!" A nasty scowl lined his piggish face. As Coach Taylor gently pushed Julie toward the door, the Alamo fan continued, "I'm sick of you pissing the season away with those dumb-ass plays . . . you will not last one year here" ("Wind Sprints," 1-3). The fan sat alone. Specks of food littered his mangy beard. Hate poured out of his eyes, and we sensed that the presence of witnesses was the only thing keeping him from hounding the Taylors all the way home.

A Panther Addict

With Buddy Garrity, *Friday Night Lights* presents yet another dysfunctional, albeit more complex and redeemable, portrait of sports fanaticism. Especially in early seasons, what Buddy wanted you to know about him, first and foremost, was his undying loyalty to the Panthers. He was "all about Panther football!" As a former Panther linebacker, Buddy presents tremendous girth. He sports a mane of wild gray hair, and his face emanates a reddish hue that implies a history of heavy drinking. And although he is often shown in a suit and tie, Buddy seems like the kind of guy who is most in his element when donning sweats and football pads.

He spent every spare moment watching the Panthers. He attended every practice, incessantly prodded Coach Taylor for inside information, and never, ever missed a Friday-night game. And during the games Buddy seemed to fall into a trancelike state, feverishly staring at the field and routinely kissing his championship ring for good luck.

The obsessive quality of these behaviors screams a simple truth: Buddy was an addict. He valued his identity as a Panther fan more than his other roles in life, and he satisfied the needs of the Panthers at the expense of his own family. He alienated his current sales team by hiring down-on-their-luck ex-Panthers, including Jason Street, and even current player Matt Saracen's father. Similarly, when his wife discovered his infidelity he had neither others' goodwill nor healthy familial habits to fall back on because he had spent all of his time and resources on the Panthers. The Taylors' household was the only place he felt he could go for emotional support and understanding, but even Coach Taylor's goodwill didn't last long. Such occupational and social impairments represent the hallmarks of addiction.

Interestingly, some of the internal forces that propelled his off-field difficulties—blurred boundaries and a tendency toward escapism—may have been the same features that predisposed and perpetuated his sports fanaticism.

Buddy struggled to effectively differentiate himself from others, to view his sense of identity clearly. In short, he lacked the wherewithal to identify the social rules that facilitate socially harmonious behavior. There were many lines in the sand that Buddy obliviously overstepped. For instance, one quickly loses count of the number of times he drove over to Coach Taylor's house, in the dead of night, to discuss a player update or a strategy for the upcoming game. His boundary problems only escalated in the context of stress. When he cheated on his wife, thereby breaking a marital boundary, he promptly invited himself over to the Taylors' house, where he proceeded to break even more relational boundaries by crashing on the couch for days on end, eating all the steak in the fridge, and poking into Coach Taylor's personal affairs. Weeks later, Buddy continued to struggle with the boundaries of his new familial role—often walking into the house that he had been kicked out of only to be predictably ejected moments later. And when his daughter Lyla asked why he had cheated, Buddy could not articulate a clear sense of his motives, subtly shifting to third person and confessing that "your dad's a sinner, a weak man" ("Ch-Ch-Ch-Ch-Changes," 1-19). And while blurred boundaries allowed him to remain disconnected from an awareness of his own actions, his ability to connect with the larger group/ideal of Panther football benefited.

Psychodynamic theory has long postulated that we as humans tend to employ defense mechanisms in response to distress in an attempt to regain a sense of safety and continuity. Ideally, we employ mature defenses that protect our sanity while guiding us toward effective problem-solving. But when Buddy's personal life collapsed, Buddy immaturely retreated into his psychological safe haven of Panther football.

In one telling scene toward the end of season one, Buddy became upset after learning that Coach Taylor had been pondering abandonment of the Panthers for a position at TMU. Buddy confronted Coach Taylor and rhetorically asked, "Don't you care at all about the Panthers?" Coach Taylor countered, "How can you even think about that stuff given the mess you're in with your family? You need to care less about who's coaching the Panthers and more about your family." In a striking display of escapism-induced denial, Buddy ignored Coach Taylor's concern and spat back, "I'll always care about the Panthers. She can cut off my head and stick it on a spike in the front lawn, but I'll always care" ("Extended Families," 1-18).

These same tendencies may have led him to spend an inordinate amount of time reexperiencing and, in turn, strengthening his Panther-related associations, even as they provided an escape from the reality of his family life. At a Panther-sponsored party early in the second season, a heavily intoxicated Buddy was seen retelling stories of championship games from decades ago with startling detail and clarity—providing play-by-play commentary of winning drives and exuding a glee on par with the original experience. For the moment, at least, the dissolution of his family that drove him to drink in the first place was held at a distance.

Sports Fanaticism As a Mental Health Cushion

But pathology is not the only outcome for sports fanatics like Buddy. While historic research and speculation sought to connect fandom with mental illness, more recent research has unearthed its hidden psychological benefits. Compared to nonfans, sports fanatics seem to experience less tension, anxiety, anger, loneliness, and depression. Moreover, increased life satisfaction, vigor, positive affect, self-esteem, and emotional stability have also been associated with fandom. Thus, cheering for a sports team may not only make us less miserable, it may make us happier. This is a far cry from the obsessive loner or the riotous crowd member, and an important question becomes, what are the specific ways in which fandom promotes mental health? While the jury is still out, one popular theory—the Team Identification-Social Psychological Health Model—points to feelings of identification with a valued group and connections with others as the likely pathway. This makes sense in light of the fact that a sense of belonging—to feel cared for and supported by others and to return the favor in kind—is a psychological need as fundamental as hunger.

As it happens, Coach Taylor's transition to the East Dillon Lions in season four seems to follow this formula. In almost every way, East Dillon pales in comparison to the town of Dillon and the championship Panther program. East Dillon is an impoverished community with fewer resources and far fewer fans. At the start of season four, the East Dillon high school had just reopened after years of dilapidation; the Lions had little history and even less on-field success. Strikingly, Coach Taylor canceled the first practice after twenty minutes out of sheer mercy, because the players were so out of shape and unprepared. The team harbored little talent, hope, or connection. Predictably, the first regular-season game unfolded in such a one-sided fashion that Coach Taylor forfeited the game at halftime. The few fans in attendance booed loudly.

Fast-forward to the end of the fourth season—and a transformation had taken place. The Lions, having become a respectable opponent, upset the rival Panthers in the final game of the season. And we watched as the Lions not only played with pride and excellence, but did so in front of a proliferating and passionate fan base. A community had been reawakened.

What happened?

As if Coach Taylor's playbook included the Team Identification-Social Psychological Health Model, a bridge of social connection between and among the fans slowly materialized. Coach Taylor dipped into his own shallow pockets to fund new uniforms for the players to proudly dirty up during games. He corralled a former Lion championship team to speak to the current Lions. He turned the lights on at Carroll Park and he initiated pep rallies and fund-raisers at East Dillon High School. Each of these steps strengthened the relationship between and among the fans, as the players uncovered a fierce motivator (the

fans) while the townspeople found a healthy means of chan-
neling the stresses and negative emotions of their private lives
(cheering for the Lions).

It should be noted that the benefits of fandom do not seem
to emerge from the simple act of rooting for a team or jumping
on a bandwagon. Surprisingly, our sense of satisfaction flows
from our relationship to other fans more than it does the team's
performance.

Buddy's transition from the Panthers to the Lions illustrates
this point perfectly.

The intense nature of Buddy's Panther addiction declined in
season three when Joe McCoy, the father of the Panthers' new
quarterback, entered the equation. Joe hijacked the booster club
and the Panther team with his seemingly endless resources and
relentlessness. In response, Buddy learned that what really drove
his sports fanaticism were his values and friendships—not the
Panthers themselves.

Buddy began to change course when his status among the
Panther in-group dipped. Whereas Coach Taylor had always
helped Buddy to stay perched high atop the Panther hierarchy,
Joe McCoy and new Panther coach Wade Aikman froze him out
of practices and meetings. Then the McCoy-led booster club
ruthlessly attacked Principal Taylor for shipping the star running
back, Luke, over to East Dillon; her car was spray painted, and
she was booed off the stage at pep rallies. In Buddy's eyes, the
morality of the Panther in-group continued to nose-dive during
the Lion-Panther rivalry week, when the Panthers responded to a
harmless prank by completely destroying the recently renovated
Lions field. The disproportionately aggressive act proved especially repugnant, as Buddy knew that East Dillon could scarcely
afford a new field, and the players had poured their sweat into its
renovation. The shift in Buddy's loyalty was finalized when he
took stock of his relationships. He realized that Coach Taylor was

his most loyal and intimate friend. Moreover, when he arrived at Coach Taylor's house to help with a new Lion booster club, he found himself face-to-face with former Lion alumni who enjoyed and appreciated Buddy's passion in ways that the Panther community had long since forgotten. Interestingly, the turning points in Buddy's transformation prove consistent with research showing that in-group allegiance (the Buddy-Panther connection) suffers when the in-group is perceived as less distinct from rival groups, as well as less successful, less morally superior, and less accepting.

Even "the town," despite the pathology it exhibited in punishing group members for endangering the status and well-being of the group, benefited from the social connection provided by fandom. A silver lining of health could be spotted weaving its way through the hostile commentary of Slammin' Sammy radio, the misguided campaigns of the booster club, even the mass drunken binges following defeats. "The town" celebrated victories and mourned defeats—together. If you were to scan the crowded Dillon stands on Friday night you might notice Matt Saracen's mother and grandmother burying the hatchet, or the ice melting between Buddy and his rebellious adolescent children. When the booster club pressured the school board for Panther-related favors, what they were really doing was seeking to preserve and enhance this unique communal space.

Further, hidden within the relational transaction between the team and its fans were additional examples of a mentally healthy life: meaningful relationships, effective coping, optimal productivity, etc. Exhibit A: the reinvigorated Lions team. To start, Coach Taylor taught the players how to live a life in line with healthy values. He instructed each player on how to foster a determined and goal-oriented attitude in practice. And throughout each week of practice an identity makeover took place. The players transformed from aimless high school nobodies to competent and appreciated teammates. As the losses piled up but became less demoralizing, Coach Taylor helped each player to function within his assigned role and to understand and rely on the roles of his teammates. This on-field learning process generalized into off-the-field success, as Vince learned to put the team ahead of gang pressure, and Tanker helped Luke build a fence. Consequently, the team's success gained traction, and the surrounding community began to see the effects of the mentally healthy magic. A Coach Taylor pregame speech to the Lions at the start of the season made this implicit process more explicit:

> Let's enjoy ourselves tonight, fellas. Because tomorrow—if you give a hundred percent of yourselves tonight—people are going to look at you differently; people are going to think of you differently, and I promise you this, gentleman—you're going to look at and feel differently about yourselves.

This moment planted the seed of a concept that grew throughout the season. The team had a job to do. They didn't just need to play fundamentally sound football and move the sticks; they needed to transform their lives and become dedicated, moral, creative, and resilient people. And as sports help transform players into mentally healthier human beings, fans may observe and internalize this transformation themselves—another potential psychological benefit to fandom.

Being a sports fan can feel almost addictive. It can provide incredible rushes, and leave us suffering surprising lows, but either way, we find ourselves unwilling, even unable, to stop. *Friday Night Lights* shines a light on sports fanaticism that shows it to be alternately negative, positive, or some mixture of both. Once the dust settles, a nuanced picture of sports fanaticism emerges—one that resembles what we know about most drugs.

If used excessively and by the wrong person, sports fanaticism may serve a destructive function that can instill bad habits and promote character weaknesses. But handled properly, sports fandom may foster a surprisingly profound degree of psychological growth and resiliency.

The same might be said of *Friday Night Lights* fanaticism, as well.

Man Up

The Football Mentality of
Friday Night Lights

KIARA KOENIG

**PEE-WEE FOOTBALL PLAYER: Mr. Street, do you think that
God loves football?
JASON STREET: I think that everybody loves football.**
— "Pilot" (1-1)

Everybody loves football, because football is America. It's teamwork and preparation, toughness and determination. It's all
about pride and defending what's ours: our house, our territory,
our family. It's about glory and respect, and leaving your mark on
the record books, on the world. It's about winning, getting paid,
and getting the girl. Football separates the men from the boys
and brings whole communities back from the brink.

Nice speech, right? But is it true?

To answer this question, *Friday Night Lights* invites us to visit
Dillon, Texas. We listen to the local sports talk shows. We meet
individuals like Jason Street, the golden boy with "NFL quarterback" written all over him; Luke Cafferty, who dreams of using

his skills as a running back to break free of the family ranch; and Jess Merriweather, the only female in a football-crazed family.

On Friday nights, we sit in Panther stadium, surrounded by family. One row over is Grandma Saracen, who spends hours helping her grandson learn the playbook. Two rows up is Smash Williams' mother, who works two jobs to keep her son on the field and off the street. Down below, stalking the sidelines and earning glares from coaches and officials, is Buddy Garrity, head booster, fund-raiser, and hell-raiser, who values his state championship ring more than his wedding ring.

We watch their dreams come true as a football falls out of the darkness and into the outstretched hands of an open wide receiver. But there's another side to this moment of triumph. As Coach Taylor puts it in the pilot episode, in football and in life, "we are all vulnerable." What we love "can be taken from us." *Friday Night Lights* doesn't pretend otherwise.

"The bigger the hit, the greater the roar."
—Buzz Bissinger,
"Texas Football and the Price of Paralysis," *Time*

Let's go back to Panther stadium, to that pass finding the receiver who crosses the goal line for the win as time expires. Rewind the tape of that game to the moment when a single play turns the abstract knowledge that football is violent and dangerous into a reality you feel in your gut, in your throat, in your heart. Watch the golden boy QB make the touchdown-saving tackle. See him lying motionless on the field. Hear the silence in the stands, the whispered prayers. Watch as Jason Street is strapped to a gurney. Follow the ambulance as it carries him toward a future unlike any he ever imagined, a future without football, without the use of his legs, without any concept of himself that makes sense. Then watch him try to figure out how to be a man, much less how to be a good man, as that future unfolds.

In its very first episode, *Friday Night Lights* staked its claim to being what *Friday Night Lights* franchise-originator Buzz Bissinger called "a show with real themes and real characters and as many dreams shattered as realized." Then, the television show spent the next five seasons exploring football from the inside out. It put us on the practice field at midnight, running shadow plays before the next game, and in Smash Williams' bedroom, staring at a syringe full of strength and speed, wondering if it's worth the risk. We sat in booster-club meetings, dissecting scouting reports on promising sixth graders and players displaced by natural disasters, figuring out what it would take to talk the parents into putting their kids in Panther uniforms. We saw the players' joy when they put on those jerseys, the pain when they set them aside or had them taken away.

"It's football. It's all we got . . . This team needs a W. This town needs a W."
  —Buddy Garrity, "Eyes Wide Open" (1-2)

As captured by scenes of kids playing youth football in miniature versions of the Dillon Panther helmets and uniforms, in towns like Dillon and its real-life inspiration, Odessa, football is both generational and communal. Jason Street tells a locker room full of star-struck youngsters to study their playbooks and listen to their coaches because in five or six years, if they're lucky, they'll be running those plays on Friday nights in front of 20,000 fans. When the Panthers play, the whole town closes its doors and posts "Gone to the Game" signs in storefront windows. Around town, every third or fourth person on the street wears a state championship ring, and the varsity players can't go anywhere without being recognized and quizzed about last week's game or next year's team.

I didn't grow up in a town like Dillon, where football is the heart of the community. I didn't attend a high school football game until I was in high school, and the great players from previous generations didn't come back to teach camps or give speeches. I loved the game, though. My dad rocked me to sleep while watching Monday Night Football. When I was five or six, he started teaching me the basics, using a game he invented called "football in the hall." The rules for this game were simple— you had four downs to make it the length of the hallway. The opposing player could tackle you or strip the ball and head in the other direction. To make it a more even match, my dad played on his knees. Even so, it was a bit like a tackling drill between a 350-pound lineman and a 180-pound wide receiver. My dad spent ten hours a day laying block, moving wheelbarrows full of cement, and carrying hundred pound bags of concrete mix. I got bounced against walls, picked up and tossed backwards down the hallway onto throw pillows, or simply pinned against the floor with one arm. I absolutely loved it.

Later, my dad taught me how to identify defenses and call plays while we watched games on Sundays, and at halftime we'd go outside and practice throwing real spirals, first to a hula hoop, then to a five-gallon bucket. In elementary school, my friends and I didn't have an actual field, so we played street ball in the evenings and in the gravel parking lot during recess. Rather than wishing for the real thing, we considered our fields a testament to our toughness. After all, anybody can play on grass, but a real player knows how to leave a defender slipping and sliding on loose gravel and doesn't mind getting

slammed into the cars parked along the "sidelines" to gain
an extra yard or two. All those games of football in the hall
taught me to fight for every inch, to make myself small to
squeeze through an opening, and to run right over any player
who was off-balance. Or, in the words of Aliquippa head
coach Mike Zminajac, to "knock the crap out of 'em—and
then help 'em up."

Are You Going to Cowboy Up or Just Lay There and Bleed
**   —T-shirt slogan**

In *The Best Game Ever*, Mark Bowden describes football as a sport
in which "courage and resilience [are] rigorously and publicly
tested," a sport that rewards "selflessness, teamwork, stamina,
discipline, and fortitude." But it is also the sport that *Sports
Illustrated*'s Frank Deford recently labeled "so physical that, for
growing boys, [it] may be no longer worth the price of admission
to manhood." Beyond the highlights and fantasy league stats,
worries about head trauma, spinal cord injuries, and the use of
performance-enhancing drugs dominate the headlines. The suicide of two-time Super Bowl champ Dave Duerson in February
of 2011 is particularly haunting because he chose to shoot himself in the chest to allow his brain to be tested for chronic traumatic encephalopathy, a degenerative brain illness linked to head
trauma in soldiers, boxers, and, increasingly, football players. In
light of stories like Duerson's and those of Andre Waters, Owen
Thomas, and so many others, at what point does being told to
"man up"—the phrase that defines the football mentality—turn
from encouragement to curse?

Over the past decade, the football term man up has become

a cultural catchphrase.[1] In a man-to-man defense, you and you alone are responsible for covering the offensive player assigned to you. It is your job to beat him off the line, to outmuscle him for the ball, to win your individual matchup on every play, so that your team can win the game. On the field, it can also translate as *stop being such a girl, and just shut up and play.* Off the field, the phrase often means *toughen up, grow a pair, take responsibility, be fearless.* Both on and off the field, it means no weakness, no quitting, no whining.

One of the best examples of how ingrained this attitude is among players comes early in season four. In his first game as head coach of the East Dillon Lions, down 47-0 at halftime and facing a locker room full of beat-up and beat-down players, Coach Taylor has to make a decision. His players swear they're good to go, that they can still play despite the icepacks and the stitches, the bruises and the bleeding. Tinker, slumped against the wall like a crash-test dummy, can't even open his eyes when asked how he's doing, yet still says he's "solid." Landry Clarke, after spitting a thick stream of dark blood onto the floor between his cleats, insists "I'm good." Diagnosed with a "hell of a high ankle sprain," Vince Howard begs, "Tell him, tell him I can still go . . . I can play" ("After the Fall," 4-2).

Coach Taylor decides to forfeit the game. His attempt to protect his players leads to a lawn full of white flags and open rebellion from the team. "Everyone gave absolutely everything that they had out there," Landry tells him when he asks why no one is showing up for practice. "And you just quit on us" (4-2). By forfeiting the game, the team believes Coach Taylor took away their chance to prove how tough they were, their chance to earn back some respect by gutting it out. And this isn't just the attitude

---

1 For more on the origins of this phrase, see Ben Zimmer's *New York Times* On Language column, "The Meaning of Man Up" (September 3, 2010).

of the young. The next week, when Coach Taylor asks for more school support, East Dillon's principal replies, "Let's see if we can finish some games before we start writing checks." Then he adds, "Either you turn it around or we shut it down" ("In the Skin of a Lion," 4-3). Even the principal is telling his coach to man up, stop whining, and start playing.

"Let's go, Luke. Suck it up. Suck it up. Walk it off."
   —Coach Taylor, "Injury List" (4-11)

As Annie Dillard writes in her autobiography, *An American Childhood*, even as a kid, the only way to play football was "all or nothing. If you hesitated in fear, you would miss and get hurt . . . Your fate, and your team's score, depended on your concentration and courage." As the stories of Cafferty and Williams make clear, you do what you have to do to get back on the field, whether that's hide an injury or take performance-enhancing drugs. Hall of Fame safety Ronnie Lott, who chose to amputate his finger rather than come out of the game, epitomizes this all-or-nothing attitude, which I bought into wholeheartedly as a kid. In third grade, when I tried to juke a defender and my hip dislocated, I used my fist to pop it back in place and kept playing. A couple of weeks later, when I fell off a horse going over a jump and my hip dislocated again, I popped it back in place and got back on the horse. I didn't tell anyone, and I certainly didn't cry. I believed I could play through it, that I could "gut it out," that it was better to hide my injury rather than admit I was hurt and have people think of me as weak or a failure.

The potential costs of this "suck it up" mentality show up frequently in *Friday Night Lights*. Early in season four, Luke Cafferty tells Coach Taylor, "I need a scholarship to a good school, so I can get out of here. That's what I need" (4-3). And "getting noticed" on the football field is his only shot. Cafferty's statement that he's "willing to kill myself, 'cause I want to get out of here, Coach," might seem like bravado, except that, after severely injuring his hip, Cafferty hides the extent of the damage through a combination of pain meds and stubbornness. He's willing to gut it out, play through the pain, and beg Oxycontin from a sympathetic doctor, or even buy it from a corner drug dealer if that's what it takes.

When Coach Taylor catches on, he yells at Cafferty, "You did that four weeks ago and you didn't tell us?" ("Injury List," 4-11). Of course not, not when admitting an injury could mean the end of a dream. Consider the case of former New England Patriots safety Rodney Harrison. Harrison, who in the space of a couple seasons tore three knee ligaments, his quadriceps, and his shoulder, admitted he took human growth hormone (HGH) to heal more quickly and get back on the field. In *Friday Night Lights*, Cafferty's use of painkillers and Smash Williams' flirtation with steroids point to the pressure to perform that even high school players feel. You don't want to let down your teammates, your coaches, or your family, especially when the stands are sprinkled with college scouts and bloggers from websites devoted to finding the next big start, filming highlights and posting tidbits from their cell phones. You do what you have to do to get back on the field, whether that's hide an injury or push the plunger on that syringe of performance-enhancing drugs. There's too much at stake not to.

Yet, when I hear the stories of ex-football players who can't bend over to tie their shoes, who can't walk without pain, who live with postconcussion symptoms, including blinding headaches and severe depression, I wonder whether being tough and playing through pain is worth it.

As neuroscientists like Dr. Ann McKee at Boston University continue to investigate the relationship between the concussive hits in football and the migraines, depression, and dementia suffered by many former players, the question may soon become, would you trade a decade or three off the end of your life for glory right now? In my case, after three months, I couldn't pound my hip back into place, and I had to tell my parents. By that point, the joint was so messed up, the doctors seriously considered amputating my leg. Instead, I had surgery, spent six months on crutches and most of my life since in pain. Was proving I wasn't "a crybaby girl" worth it? Yes. And no.

"But she won't stop. She'll collect herself and keep going. She's relentless."

—Folsom coach Mike Collier, "Too Short for Football, She Stands Tall in Adopted Sport," *Sacramento Bee*

I grew up knowing there was no more deadly insult than "you play like a girl." Girls were wimps who threw wobbly passes and were scared to tackle. That perception is changing, thanks to young women like Folsom High School's Tiana Camous, who played youth football and joined the junior varsity team. Camous gave up football because she stopped growing, not because she had a "problem with the hitting or tackling." Even so, there's still no female equivalent for man up. What are you going to say, "Grow a bigger pair of ovaries," or, "Tighten your bra-straps"?

And yet, in life and on *Friday Night Lights*, some of the best examples of the "football mentality" done right are female. Take Jess Merriweather, for example. Unlike most of the rally girls and cheerleaders, she doesn't kowtow to the football players or go to the games just because her boyfriend is playing. She may not play, but she understands the game. We see it when she teaches Landry how to punt, and we hear it when she's coaching her brother Caleb on how to stop the sweep. She knows football because her father used to play, because her three younger brothers love to play, and because she loves the game. When she tells her father, "We're still a football family," she says it with pride ("A Sort of Homecoming," 4-4).

Yet, because she's not out on the field making tackles or scoring touchdowns, she struggles to earn respect from those whose lives are defined by the gridiron. One of the show's most powerful scenes occurs after Vince asks Jess's father, Big Mary, for money. While Jess listens from the hallway, Big Mary tells Vince how proud he is of him. After Vince leaves, Jess asks her father why he's willing to go watch Vince practice when he won't come to watch his own sons play. Then, fighting tears, she asks why he doesn't come to watch her dance or support her when she competes in academic smack-downs. "I try really hard to make you proud, too," she tells him ("I Can't," 4-10).

The scene highlights how the brightness of the stadium lights can leave so many good things hidden in the shadows and so many good people unrecognized and unappreciated. Big Mary should be proud of Jess. She's tough, smart, and responsible. When Landry runs over her bike, she refuses to back down, insisting he pay for the damages. She does well in school. She takes care of nearly everyone else in her life, as if they were all part of her team. She visits Vince's mom in rehab, makes sure her brothers get to school and practice, and works for her dad at the barbeque joint. What more could a parent want?

In many ways, Jess is a younger version of Tami Taylor, another smart, funny, strong-willed woman whose life is defined by football. Being the coach's wife is a thankless job. At a book-club meeting in season one, the only topic of conversation is how her husband should coach the game, including one mother's insistence that the team won't win unless her son plays more. When Tami takes over as principal, the boosters threaten her when she tries to give funds to anything other than the football team. After Dillon is forced to redistrict, she's booed at pep rallies and snubbed at church for insisting that even the football players must attend their assigned high school. Yet, whether she's throwing a last-minute party for the entire town, arguing that academic pursuits are just as deserving of investment as the football team, or facing down angry boosters and parents, football players everywhere could learn from Tami's toughness and grace under pressure.

"There are only two paths left for football: acceptance or abolishment."
   —Buzz Bissinger, "NFL Playoffs: Why Football Needs Violence," the *Daily Beast*

I'll be honest. Like many Dillon residents and sports talk show callers, I'm a slightly crazy, superstitious fan. I use first person when talking about "my" teams, including myself in the agony or the celebration by describing what we did or didn't do. During close games, my hands shake, my throat closes up, and my heart hiccups. I have no patience for those who don't watch the game with the same single-minded focus I do, and losses can still leave me irritable for hours afterward. The best of the game scenes in *Friday Night Lights* have the same impact on me that a real game does. Even now, watching the pilot episode for the fourth or fifth time, my throat gets tight when Street lays motionless on the turf, and I get goose bumps when Saracen flings that game-winning pass downfield.

As captured so effectively in the juxtaposition of images from the game and the hospital in the very first episode, the series has been steadfast in its insistence on capturing both the beauty of football and its flaws. At its heart, football is a violent sport, and, while I feel guilty admitting it, the violence is part of why I love it. I still remember how good it felt to get a solid hit on a ball carrier. I still remember how good it felt to win. Maybe Dennis Byrd, who was paralyzed from the waist down during an NFL game in 1992 but regained the use of his legs a year later, said it best in a recent interview: "[I] would trade everything that I had for one more game and one more play."

Friday Night Lights reminds us that this game is played by human beings, not robots or gods, that what happens off the field can both influence and be redeemed by what happens on the field, and that there are consequences to our actions. I believe that football still has the potential to bring out the best in us individually and to inspire us as a community. For that to happen, we need to insist on a football mentality that defines courage as toughness mixed with common sense; that defines excellence as hard work, discipline, and intelligence, not just wins; that focuses on the skills of the individual, not just the stats of the player. The legacy of *Friday Night Lights* is the conviction that, regardless of gender, football has the power to create better people, not just bigger, faster, stronger players at any cost.

From *The Washington Post's*
Jen Chaney

WHY WE LOVE

. . . Jess Merriweather

We didn't get to know Jess Merriweather as well as we would have liked. After all, the surrogate mother to three misbehaving brothers didn't join *Friday Night Lights* until season four. And in many of those episodes, she sometimes felt like more of a pretty narrative convenience, a set of dimples and a wide, warm smile designed by the writers to anchor a (mostly) believable love triangle involving Landry Clarke and Vince Howard.

But during season five, Jess blossomed into a multidimensional young woman, a sort of combo platter of Tyra Collette's feistiness, Lyla Garrity's femininity, and Matt Saracen's über-responsibility. While often parenting her three little brothers, she continued to work at her dad's barbecue joint, acted as romantic partner and voice of reason to Vince, and, most importantly, became equipment manager for the East Dillon Lions.

That last job was the most significant one for Jess because it led her to the role of pseudoassistant to Coach Taylor and closer to realizing her own coaching dream. A former dance team member, ditching those moves for the world of play-calling, locker room talk, and the smell of man-sweat? Absolutely. Jess Merriweather did that happily, for the love of the game.

And for that reason, as well as the ones listed below, we love Jess Merriweather.

- She was the kind of girl who would make an iPod playlist for Landry, one that consisted solely of crowd noise so he could get psyched up while he practiced kicking.
- She was honest enough to tell Landry, bluntly, that she had feelings for Vince, even though she knew it would break his heart.
- When skanky redheaded rally girl Maura flirted with Vince, Jess was not afraid to do what it took to affirm her position as the QB's girlfriend. And by "do what it took," what we mean is "chug beer through a funnel."
- She had no qualms about telling Vince when he seemed self-involved in a TV interview, or outright dumping him— "We're done, jackass"—when he morphed into someone ridiculously arrogant.
- Given her ability to clandestinely secure footage of rival teams, break down plays, and know why someone is jumping the snap count, she proved to be a better assistant coach than anyone on Coach Taylor's Lions crew . . . and yes, obviously we're including Stan Traub.
- Jess proved that some girls just look better—more right—in shorts, an East Dillon polo shirt, and a red baseball cap than they do in spandex dance team wear.
- Our young, aspiring molder of men was convinced that because a woman became the coach of a high school football team in Washington, DC, she could someday do it, too. And so were we.

The football portions of *Friday Night Lights* are most often about boys being boys and trying to be men. Unlike the romances and the family relationship plotlines, they are all "guy stuff." Jess

Merriweather inserted herself into that world and proved that a girl belongs there, too.

The last time we saw her on *Friday Night Lights*, she was in Dallas, cap on her head, clipboard in hand, state championship ring on her finger. She was on the sidelines and very much part of the game.

WHY WE LOVE
. . . Landry Clarke

L andry Clarke killed a man.

As much as we fans would like to ignore that fact and pretend it never happened, there it is. He did it for a completely justifiable reason: to get better ratings for a beloved but little-watched TV show called *Friday Night Lights*.

No, seriously, he did it for a justifiable reason: to protect Tyra Collette, the woman he loved, from a man who was trying to attack her.

But that willingness to go all vigilante with a metal pipe—after just popping into the store for some Pringles, no less—is not the reason we love Landry Clarke. Actually, we love Landry Clarke in spite of all the melodrama that resulted from that season-two incident.

Landry Clarke was supposed to be the sidekick, the funny best friend who shows up at the Alamo Freeze at precisely the moment a sarcastic comment is required. He was supposed to be the provider of comic relief, as well as the provider of rides home when Tyra needed them, and the provider of Grandma babysitting when Matt Saracen needed that, and the provider of tutoring when Tim Riggins really needed to process *Of Mice and Men*.

He was supposed to be the guy that the football coach would forever mistakenly refer to as Lance.

But that's not who Landry Clarke ended up being. He was far more complicated and forthright, loyal and hilarious, kindhearted and, yes, heroic than that.

We love Landry Clarke because he refuses to tolerate a defeatist attitude from anyone, whether it's an indecisive Saracen or a lazy Tim Riggins, a self-doubting Tyra Collette or a confused Eric Taylor. Because he's blunt, stubborn, hilarious, and the most intelligent kid in Dillon, Texas. Because he made sure that, damn it, Coach Taylor realized his name was Landry.

For all these reasons, and the litany of additional ones listed below, we love Landry Clarke.

- Landry veers dangerously close to looking like Matt Damon but is just a little too pale and nerdy to fully resemble him. He's either too humble or strangely unaware of Mr. Damon's filmography to ever bother pointing this out.
- Landry not only dared to be the frontman for a band named Crucifictorious, he actually expected a packed house at their first gig.
- He never hesitates to offer candid advice, even when that advice means idiotically encouraging his best friend, Matt, to "pull out the big guns" by wearing a Members Only jacket on a first date.
- Our Landry is an expert on a wide variety of subjects and is always eager to dispense his sage advice on any matter, including fashion (see above), the appropriate moment to give a girl a mix tape, condom choices, literary analysis, and how to handle being on the wait list at the University of Texas.
- Landry has Christian values, but also enough common sense to genuinely believe the acronym WWRD—What Would Riggins Do?—could serve as a valuable touchstone in various scenarios. (For the record, it does.)
- He managed to attract the attention of not just one but two super-cute indie-rock chicks: Jean and Devin. The latter turned

out to be a lesbian (she and Landry remained friends), but that doesn't diminish the fact that he's capable of earning the admiration of women who love *Mystery Science Theater* and the Flaming Lips—which makes Landry the hippest dude in Dillon.

- Landry had the audacity to love Tyra Collette, a girl who technically resided in Dillon, Texas, but possessed a body that existed in some *Maxim* magazine–sponsored fantasy land. He had the even greater audacity to firmly believe he would eventually become her boyfriend. And most audacious of all? He actually did.

- When Tyra expressed a desire to go back in time and kill the person who invented algebra, Landry noted that "that's kind of a Catch-22, though, because in order to invent that time machine you may need to use algebra." Only someone totally awesome says things like that.

- Landry speaks his mind, even when that means telling Coach Taylor—you know, the guy who once harbored the delusion that Landry's name was Lance—that the East Dillon Lions lost faith in their coach because he forfeited a game, betraying his lack of faith in them.

- When "waiting like a British foot soldier" for Tyra, who'd gone off to college, didn't pan out, our kicker went for another very pretty girl: Jess Merriweather. And when it became apparent that her torch was lit for someone else— new QB1 Vince Howard—he was man enough to step aside with grace.

A certain catchphrase became a motivational mantra for the Dillon Panthers long before Landry Clarke clinched a spot on the team. And yet it's Landry—perhaps more than any other *Friday Night Lights* character—who most often lived by its words.

No one's eyes were consistently clearer than Landry Clarke's. No one's heart was consistently fuller than Landry Clarke's.

And as he proved again in season four, when he emerged as the kicker capable of sending a football soaring through the goal post and earning a desperately needed East Dillon win, Landry Clarke simply couldn't lose.

Things felt immediate on this show: There was no distance between the residents of Dillon and us. In ways we'll be appreciating for years to come, [*Friday Night Lights*] consistently created a bond of empathy and compassion between the people on the screen and the people on the couch. Like few other shows, it was able to create incredibly potent emotional states that reached right into your gut and heart; it depicted and induced happiness and sadness and many inarticulate states in between.

It's only appropriate that the show, which focused so intently on the connections that sustain people in good times and in bad, created such a powerful bond between audience and characters. So often it felt that we weren't just observing them, we were *with* them. Maybe, sometimes, we *were* those people. The catharsis came from seeing ourselves on that screen—celebrated, recognized, frustrated, angry . . .

That last shot of everyone watching Vince's long pass was a perfect way to end the game. What was in their eyes wasn't just a desire to win. What shone on their faces was hope—something that is, at times, in short supply in Dillon. But that's what the game does for those Dillon residents—and that's what this show did for us. It made us part of something bigger, part of something that could break our hearts and make our eyes well up. The game on Friday gave them an outlet for their hopes, fears and frustrations. And through the fly-on-the-wall depictions of the people playing and watching that game, we felt those emotions too. The game, and the show, gave us something to look forward to and celebrate.

—**Maureen Ryan**, "Full Hearts: A Review of the 'Friday Night Lights' Series Finale," Stay Tuned with Maureen Ryan on TVSquad.com

Playing for Now

TRAVIS STEWART

Matt Saracen, feared QB1 of the state champion Dillon Panthers, is about as physically unimpressive as anyone you've ever seen.

He's short. Thin. He sports something between a stutter and a stammer, and his broken-wing throwing motion looks like he's releasing the ball with collapsible tent poles for arms. All in all, he's about as imposing as a corn tortilla.

And yet, with zeroes on the clock against rival Arnett Mead and the Panthers trailing by just a point in season one of *Friday Night Lights*, Saracen, weighing his options between a game-tying extra point and a game-winning two-point conversion, simply smiled.

"We got 'em right where we want 'em," Saracen told his coach.

No stutter. No hesitancy. No awkwardness. Just Saracen, his coach, and the game, and the very reason why the state of Texas—and now a national audience—has grown to so passionately love this common-man, Joe America pastime that fills stadiums all across our proud plains each Friday night.

Panther head coach Eric Taylor echoed Saracen's sly smile, called in the play—double-checking with the sophomore signal-caller to make sure he even understood it—and then turned over the fate of the game (and possibly his career, as Slammin' Sammy Meade suggested[1]) into the hands of . . .

Well, a corn tortilla with a stutter. That, folks, is what high school football is all about. Matt Saracen, in all of his gangly glory, is the very essence of it.

Despite popular opinion, high school football is not Brian "Smash" Williams. Some of his accompanying plotlines—battling the mental side effects of serious injury, for example, or desperately reaching for a future that can provide for an overwhelmed family—accurately portray some of the drama inherent in the sport. But Smash the player does not. Neither does pre-injury Jason Street. Tim Riggins? Vince Howard? No. To all of them. Anyone who suggests such dynamic playmakers embody the essence of high school football simply does not understand the scope of the game. Not even close.[2]

Do you know how many football-playing high schools there are in the state of Texas? More than 1,300. Even if we just take

---

1 The media takes an unbelievable beating in this TV series. At no point is any journalist portrayed in a positive light. Meade is really just an over-opinionated radio hack, and the TV and newspaper beat reporters are constantly just fishing for spicy quotes that they can present out of context. I felt like this was a pretty unfair representation—journalists care about the sport as much as anyone.

2 I do, however, fear the fine line we walk with J.D. McCoy and his ilk. The money inherent in high-level football has gotten so alluring that parents are starting to push their kids to dangerous degrees in order to mold them into future pros. Look, I know a pro QB can make $20 million a year in the NFL. But hiring a private coach for a fourteen-year-old? Damn. If the kid can make the conscious choice that that's what he wants at that age, then fine. But how many can?

the starters from those teams (we'll say twenty-two per squad, for the sake of argument), that's 28,600 players. How many of those do you really think are Smash? Or Riggins? Maybe a couple hundred?[3]

I can tell you right now, with the authority vested in me by managing *Dave Campbell's* Texas Football, the publication known in these parts as The Bible, that the overwhelming majority of those 28,000 footballers are Matt Saracen. And it's the most beautiful thing in the world.

High school ball isn't a clean game. I'd never argue that. You're going to have ugly interceptions—Saracen had his fair share, for sure. You're going to have penalties, fumbles, bad punts, and shanked extra points. If we took the outward appearance of high school football and somehow transformed it into a woman, she wouldn't turn heads on the average city street.

In other words, this is an inner-beauty sport. The glory of the game isn't in the box score, and, as *Friday Night Lights* so perfectly portrayed to us, neither is Saracen's glory in his statistics. It's in the things that can't be measured, like passion. That, to me, is the most captivating thing about both the show and the sport: it leads with its heart. While season one's state semifinal against Westerby—the Mud Bowl—wasn't realistic in the setting *Friday Night Lights* provided (postseason venues, for example, are required to provide a reasonable amount of seating for the expected audience[4]; such a jury-rigged solution would never

---

3 The state of Texas regularly puts out around 300 to 350 Football Bowl Subdivision (the big colleges, in other words) signees every year and is almost always tops in the nation. Even if we spread those stars out as fairly as possible (which isn't the case in the real world), that'd be roughly one college player for one in every four Texas high schools. Not good odds.

4 This UIL-mandated rule started in 2006, a year after Highland Park fans protested the selection of Rose Stadium in Tyler for a 4A-DI state title game because it was supposedly too small to accommodate their large fan following. Now, disputes over a selected stadium's seating capabilities are

fly in a major state semifinal), it's deliciously feasible in theory. Among some of the state's smaller schools, rules are a little more relaxed. Coach Taylor and the Panthers went out and played on a pretty standard small-town Texas field for one night, just with a little weather mixed in.

Where else in the football world would you find something like that?

While you're searching, where else would you find someone like Saracen? Where else would you find someone who's playing the game not for money or fame, but for just the sheer joy of playing it?

There have definitely been some unlikely heroes at the higher levels of football; you can bombard me with tales of undersized, overhearted success stories in the college and professional ranks from now 'til kingdom come, but what's not debatable is that those against-all-odds tearjerkers—like, say, Doug Flutie—were flanked by mind-numbing talent. In college football, most starters were high school stars. A pretty good number have the talent (if not the fortitude) to make football a career. Almost all of them were recruited to campus with that expectation.

But in high school football, the talent isn't always there. As a matter of fact, it's usually not. Kids aren't playing for futures. Or paychecks. Scholarships? Kids at some schools are lucky to get new jerseys. The simple truth is that high school football, regardless of where in America you follow it, is the last step of the road for most of its players. For Saracen.

Did we ever hear Saracen talk about picking up a scholarship to play ball anywhere? Did anyone besides Lorraine, his darling but misguided grandmother, even consider it at any point in time? Not even close. Even Julie Taylor, the one person who is

---

resolved by the UIL. Coach Taylor's idea for the cow pasture was cute, but it wouldn't have worked.

always supposed to believe in Saracen, laughed off the notion at one point.

Now that doesn't mean the kid doesn't want to fight for his time in the sun. Part of his strained relationship with Smash in season two was predicated on bruised ego: Saracen feared Smash's selfish attitude was hurting the team dynamic, which was savvy of him to pick up on. But he was also fuming that his role as a star player was withering under the glare of Smash's garish behavior. That, too, is a pretty common occurrence. Teenage personalities are going to clash, and Saracen is no saint. But for the most part, he looks like he gets the underlying principle of what it means to be a leader—though his football career isn't going anywhere in the long term, he still sees the potential to build something special in the little time he has.

No, Saracen was never playing for the future. That bony boy was always playing for Now.

Now—it's the tense most high school players are forced to focus on. Sure, Smash was locked in on the future. For a brief stint, so was Riggins. Vince Howard was nearly devoured by the notion. And once Smash finally got his crack at Texas A&M, he was probably just as focused on the next step, playing in the NFL. Even when Smash hit his lowest point, a three-game suspension for punching out a kid who had it coming, one of his first thoughts was losing his scholarship. The reality of missing the key stretch of the season certainly dawned on him, but not with the same crushing weight as the threat of losing his future.

But for Saracen, and for the thousands of players in the real world that he represents, all there is on that field is Now. There is no tomorrow. There is only this play, this game; the fine line between winning and losing that creates the most singular (and endearing) element of high school football—pure, unbridled passion.

There were many breathtaking moments in *Friday Night Lights'* five riveting seasons, but nothing gave me goose bumps more than Saracen's defining line in season three's "How the Other Half Lives" (3-3). Beaten, bloodied, and clearly pissed off, a warrior-like Saracen, exhausted from an otherworldly performance against Arnett Mead, sat on the sideline as the Panthers once again fell behind with under two minutes to play. Coach Taylor, knowing he was probably only going to get one more chance to win the thing, approached his gritty quarterback with tight lips.

COACH TAYLOR: You got one more in you?
SARACEN: I always got one more.

Those steely eyes, blood running down his face . . . that's a whole different side of Saracen, isn't it? Such a moment has played out on college and pro sidelines before, but few, if any, have done so without the battered hero playing for something more than just Now. Sure, they'd have "one more"—one more for the scholarship they're looking for, or one more for the next max-money contract. One more with another stepping-stone at the end of the effort.

But Saracen? Saracen's gut check is pure. All he wants is a win. That's it. He wants the Now. And all across Texas, every Friday night, countless teenagers are playing their hearts out for the simple joy of just competing. It's a breath of fresh air, and one the choking smog of big-money athletics all too often masks. Like Saracen's need for victory, nowhere is the sport of football as pure—in its highs or its lows—as it is in the high school ranks.

Case in point: rewatch the twelfth episode of season three, when the Panthers fall in gut-wrenching fashion to a stacked South Texas team in the state finals. Up went the Titans' game-winning field goal attempt, and down went Dillon's season. We're shown the striking dichotomy of the two teams' reactions from above, we get a close-up of a shell-shocked coach Taylor, and then we cut to a stone-silent locker room. You can almost smell that stale, flat sweat mixed with the tang of blood and grass. You can almost reach out and touch the ripped, damp nylon of the blue and white jerseys.

But the producers did forget one thing. They forgot the tears.

Have you ever seen a high school team lose a state title game? It's emotional devastation at it's most biting level, and it turns warriors into wrecks—players, coaches, parents, even beat writers lose their composure when that seventeen-week dream comes to a crashing halt. I have lost games before at that age, and I know I was broken. I promise you the Dillon locker room would have been a symphony of suffering, and there wouldn't have been a dry eye in the house.[5] That's high school football—pure football—where the emotional investment from the players is still strong enough to take them to the highest of peaks and the lowest of valleys.

Men don't cry in college ball. They don't cry in pro ball. You may get a weepy guy occasionally, but rarely more than one or two, even in the toughest of losses. It's just not the same as it is in high school ball. Part of that is because the players are older and more emotionally mature. But most of it is that the emotional investment simply isn't the same. Matt Saracen, who puts everything into the Now, is not in that locker room. His feeling of loss is so much more poignant than those players with a football future. Would you weep as hard if you knew there was still going to be a tomorrow? Saracen's final high school game—the state finals against South Texas—was the highest and lowest point of his career; playing in a state final was incredible, and then losing

---

5 My wife won't even watch the end of big-time high school games. The sheer rawness of the emotion is too much for her. Her brother, an outstanding high school player, lost a one-point state title game in his senior year. She's lived it. He played in college, too, but she has no problem seeing an FBS team lose. Doesn't that tell us something?

it was incredibly devastating. But college guys, and pro guys, and even big-name high school recruits, know their career will stretch on. Saracen knows his will not. That's going to trigger an emotional response.

And when the emotion is at its highest, isn't that pretty much the pinnacle of sporting? Isn't that, as fans, what we should be striving to support? In an age where NFL owners and players can't agree on how to divide billions of dollars, watching Saracen just plain give a damn is a thing of beauty. And it's not just the passion of a high school player like Saracen that deserves appreciation. It's how that passion affects the outcome of games. In season three's "Game of the Week" (3-9), Saracen got his number called on a fourth-and-seven with a narrow lead hanging in the balance. Not only did he catch the ball, he broke a tackle and shed another one long enough to stretch the pigskin out for a game-winning first down. Just like in the game against Arnett Mead two years before, when Saracen's two-point conversion call earned the Panthers a victory, Coach Taylor threw his little corn tortilla of a player into the pressure cooker of the moment—and the kid came out a best-in-show enchilada.

The transformation seems unbelievable. But not too long ago, a former high school and college football star sat in my kitchen and told me that, many times in his career, he did things on the field he knew he wasn't physically capable of. His body rose to the occasion, and he did what was necessary. Heart and passion lie at the root of that. Talent can only take you so far; your desire can take you much further.

Skinny little Saracen is a classic example of that, and so is his equally unimposing friend Landry Clarke. When Clarke's team needed him against Westerby in season two's "Let's Get it On" (2-5), he made winning plays all night long. And, of course, let's not forget his seminal moment in season four—trailing now-hated Dillon High with seconds left on the clock, Coach Taylor called

Clarke over for a last-second forty-six-yard field goal attempt that would end East Dillon's season on a winning note.

Clarke made no bones about his inability to do what was asked of him. Coach asked anyway. And Clarke, against even his own expectations, delivered. In high school football, that kind of minor miracle is so much more common. When college players succeed, there's no miracle, because they believed in themselves already. You don't start at the college football level unless you're confident. But high school kids are still emotionally fragile enough to show self-doubt, and when they do something incredible, like Clarke making that field goal, it's that much more astounding. Saracen's life is almost overflowing with doubt—from his lengthy battle with McCoy for the starting job he worked so hard for, to the emotionally trying confession to coach Taylor that everyone he cared about had abandoned him,[6] there was no reason for Saracen to ever really believe in himself. Even his father, in his brief return to Dillon, told Taylor—with Saracen standing right there—that he never thought his son had it in him to succeed.

But sometimes, when the pressure of the moment reaches a fever pitch, that ugly, mental wall in the teenage athlete's mind crumbles—all the crippling doubt, all the paralyzing fear . . . it all just melts away, and the result is a scintillating performance that leaves us breathless. The fuel for that transformation is simple—the knowledge that, at least in Saracen's case, the clock is ticking. There is no future in football. It's this moment, or never again. If I don't make this play, I'll never get another chance to be on the field. Modern science swears that the human body, when faced with its own demise, is capable of the most astonishing of physical feats. For the kid who's grinding away on the practice field at 6:00 a.m. every morning for four straight years, is the prospect of playoff elimination really so different?

---

6 This was without question the most painful part of the entire series. It was as emotionally gripping as any TV scene I can remember.

I know Dillon's epic comebacks in the state title games in both season one and season three are hard to fathom, but I assure you I've seen crazier things.[7] When kids know that this moment could be their last . . . the brain stops, and the heart takes over.

Every year, almost every playoff team in Texas will lose, and 99 percent of those teams will bid good-bye to their seniors at the final whistle. The simple truth is that when Saracen's Herculean effort fell short against South Texas, we watched a death as emotionally riveting as that of his father's in season four: the death of his football career.

Interestingly enough, *Friday Night Lights* did an excellent job of conveying the finality of an individual's high school existence—not with tears, but with departures. When it finally came time for Smash to move on to A&M, we saw his face in dramatic slow-mo, flashing that familiar smile, to end season three's "Hello, Good-bye" (3-4) . . . and then he was gone, for good. When Lyla Garrity and Tyra Collette both left for college, we saw each of them once or twice in the final two seasons, but, for the most part, they had moved on. And Street, once he finally found a way to be with the woman and son he missed so much, took his leave, as well.

But we never quite left Matt Saracen, did we? Unlike most of the other original players, his story remained central to *Friday Night Lights*. His football career was dead. His on-field glory days were far behind him. But our emotional investment in

---

7 The most astonishing sporting event I've ever seen in person was San Antonio Madison high school's fourth-quarter comeback against Smithson Valley in the 2007 football playoffs. Madison trailed 28 to 7 to start the fourth quarter and won in overtime, 38 to 35. This game proved my point about five times over in a ten-minute span. A year later, Prosper, a smaller school in Texas, battled back to down Abilene Wylie in a double-overtime state semifinal through a seemingly impossible last-second drive. A week later, Prosper went on to win the state title after trailing most of the first half 10 to 0. Every time I discuss this theory, I think of the green and white of the Prosper Eagles.

the underdog hero was simply too great to discard, just like his emotional investment in the game eventually took him from the bench to wide receiver. The kid loved the game, and for that, we loved him.

And because of him, and players like him, we love high school football.

WHY WE LOVE
. . . Matt Saracen

It was never, ever easy being Matt Saracen.

As a high school sophomore, he had to act as the head of his household and caretaker to a grandmother suffering from dementia. He held down a part-time job dishing out burgers and soft-serve ice cream at the Alamo Freeze while keeping up with his studies and continuing to pursue his interest in art. He was forced to listen to the relentless unsolicited advice offered by his best friend, Landry Clarke, and to tolerate the mood swings of his often melodramatic girlfriend, Julie Taylor. And on top of all that, he had to deal with the pressure of being thrust from backup QB to QB1 after the dean of Dillon Panthers football, Jason Street, suffered a devastating injury.

Somehow Saracen handled all of this responsibility with admirable maturity and a loving heart. Also, briefly, with a tendency to hook up with his grandma's improbably hot live-in Guatemalan nurse.

Look, Matt Saracen was only human, okay? He had flaws. For starters, he was a mumbler. Seriously, count the times you had to rewind your DVR because you couldn't quite make out what the heck Saracen just said. The total is somewhere in triple digits, isn't it?

He sometimes made mistakes, too, like getting drunk with Tim Riggins in the middle of the day, or going to Chicago without returning

Julie's calls, or having his picture taken in a hot tub with some rally girls, then pretending that he didn't.

Still, no one on *Friday Night Lights* generated more well-earned empathy than Matt Saracen. No one else so frequently deserved a huge, reassuring hug. And no one made us—yes, even the stoic, manly men among us—shed so many tears.

When Saracen sat fully clothed in the shower and asked Coach Taylor why everyone in his life always left him, our hearts broke. When he wrestled through sobs with the anger, sadness, and resentment that followed his father's death in Iraq, our hearts shattered entirely.

Matt Saracen was an adequate quarterback who showed occasional flashes of brilliance.

But as the boyfriend who wanted to have sex only when he and Julie were ready; the quarterback who kept his eyes wide open and threw the long touchdown pass when it really counted; the prince of a grandson who swept his grandma out of a nursing home and onto a dance floor; and the young man who knew, beyond a doubt, that he wanted to marry Julie Taylor, Matt Saracen was something really, really special.

We love him because of all that. And because of these reasons, too.

- Saracen is the rare high school quarterback who loves calling plays, but loves Jackson Pollock just as much.
- In the Alamo Freeze parking lot, before throwing the first punch in a fight with several members of the rival Arnett Mead team, Saracen was polite enough to offer them all complimentary Swizzlers.
- Saracen naively believed that dropping his name at the local multiplex—"I'm Matt Saracen, QB1 for the Dillon Panthers"—would score him a free pair of tickets to *Eragon*.

- When his grandma suffered from a mental episode and locked herself in the closet, Saracen didn't hesitate to adopt the voice of his late grandfather Joel and coax her out by singing "Mr. Sandman"—simultaneously one of the creepiest and most poignant moments from the past decade of television.

- This introspective, often insecure, perpetually apologetic kid somehow found the balls to tell Coach Taylor that he planned to date his daughter, and that there was nothing Coach could do to stop it.

- Instead of having sex with Julie in a cabin as planned, Saracen spent the night leg wrestling with her. He capped off that romantic occasion by telling Julie: "You have the ugliest feet I have ever seen."

- After dumping Lauren, the cute new girl at Dillon, then getting dumped by Carlotta—the aforementioned improbably hot live-in nurse—Saracen proved that he should star in his own rom-com: "How to Lose Two Girls in Less than 10 Episodes."

- While enjoying a pitcher of beer in the middle of the day with Riggins, the ever-suave Saracen greeted born-again Christian couple Lyla Garrity and Chris Kennedy by waving and—for reasons that defy explanation in English as well as Hebrew—saying "Shalom."

- After being benched as QB in favor of that little weasel J.D. McCoy, Saracen didn't hesitate to accept a challenge from Coach Taylor: nail ten drills, in the street in front of the Taylors' house, and he would get the opportunity to play wide receiver. Saracen impressively caught nine out of ten passes. As always, not perfect, but enough to earn the respect of his coach.

- Our former QB had the heart to forgive the mom who regretted leaving him when he was a child. He had the heart to do the hard but right thing by placing his grandma in a nursing home where she would have twenty-four-hour care. And he had the heart to do the harder, even righter thing: mend fences between the woman who raised him and the woman who should have raised him so they could be there for each other.
- Is Saracen actually a talented artist? We suspect he is. At the very least, we know this much: that kid can draw one hell of a human hand on sketch paper.
- Saracen got down on one knee and proposed to Julie— offering her his grandma's ring (awwww)—in the most meaningful of places: outside the Alamo Freeze, the same burger joint where Smash Williams once gave Saracen advice about his first sexual experience with Julie.
- In yet another ballsy move, Saracen made sure that Coach Taylor knew that he was only asking for his blessing to propose to Julie "as a courtesy."

During season one, when Coach Taylor took Saracen out for a late-night pep talk on the Dillon High football field, we saw the birth of this kid's confidence. Suddenly, he was shouting out plays—without mumbling, it should be noted—and throwing the football like he was launching a NASA missile.

"Your dad's not able to see what I see," Coach told him then. "I believe you can do anything you put your mind to."

Three seasons later, after Matt had buried his father, he got into a car and hit the road for Chicago. And that's when we saw the full realization of that confidence, and the realization of some well-earned freedom. For the first time in Matt Saracen's life, it looked like things—finally, mercifully, deservedly—just might get a little easier. And later, when Matt decided to spend the rest of his life with Julie, things looked like they just might eventually be perfect.

WHY WE LOVE

. . . Vince Howard

Vince Howard became Coach Eric Taylor's most daunting challenge. A kid with a criminal record, a drug-addicted mother, a dad in jail, and a tendency to hang with some super-shady dudes, young Vince had little genuine interest in playing football, much less becoming leader of his high school team.

But become its leader, and its state championship–winning quarterback, is exactly what Vince Howard did. A wiry teen with a perpetually determined look on his face and a world of problems on his shoulders, Vince, while occasionally cocky, didn't display the kind of joyful arrogance we saw in Smash Williams. He wasn't as quotable as the pithy Tim Riggins. And while, like Matt Saracen, he had responsibilities at home that forced him to become a man before he finished being a boy, Vince wasn't the kind of character who made us yearn to give him a hug.

Vince was all toughness and hard lessons, promising athlete and beyond-loyal son, the kid who squeaked out of going to juvie and soared like a well-thrown football in flight once he became an East Dillon Panther. We loved him because he overcame his surroundings.

And we also loved him because:

- When Coach Taylor gave Vince's strung-out mom $20 and looked every inch the patronizing, postracism-era white male while doing it, Vince returned the cash. From minute one, the kid had his pride.

- While complaining about Coach Taylor's aggressive coaching, Vince once referred to him as a "white boy." As in, "That white boy sucks." Coach Taylor is many things, white among them. But boy?

- He broke our hearts when he sat by his mother's hospital bed after her overdose, a self-assured young man suddenly transformed into a scared little boy who couldn't bear to go on without his mom.

- Vince had the class to give Landry Clarke his blessing when it appeared he was winning Jess' heart: "You're a good dude. And Jess deserves the best. I'm glad you two are together."

- Vince had the common sense to run like hell rather than fire a gun in retaliation against the people who killed his friend Calvin.

- Unlike his dad, Vince knew when it was time to step back from untrustworthy college recruiters and get back in line with the coach who gave him a break when the only thing he knew about football was how to play *Madden*.

- When he finally dropped his "I'm a top recruit" arrogance, he was gentlemanly enough to let Jess know he was happy to have his girlfriend, the equipment manager, be part of the team.

He didn't forget to thank the people who helped him succeed, especially his coach. "I don't know where I would be without you," he told Coach Taylor while standing in his front yard. "Either in jail or in a ditch somewhere."

Vince Howard didn't end up in a jail or in a ditch somewhere. He ended up, as the final *Friday Night Lights* montage tells us, playing quarterback for the superteam version of the Dillon Panthers. He had a championship ring on his finger. And he was playing under the tutelage of Coach Spivey, the former assistant who apparently rose up to become the first black coach in Dillon Panther history. Vince Howard was exactly where he belonged.

Viewers Wanted
(Teens Need Not Apply)

ROBIN WASSERMAN

There are, I am told, people out there in the cultural universe who are more than willing to accept—perhaps even encourage—the existence of tastes and proclivities that differ from their own.

Fair warning: I am not one of those people.

When I like something, and I mean *really* like it, I tend to find it inexplicable when the rest of the world doesn't feel the same way.[1] And suffice it to say, I like *Friday Night Lights* a *lot*. So you can imagine I've logged more than a few hours trying to figure out why it wasn't the top-rated show on television, why it didn't sweep the Emmys on an annual basis, why it wasn't mandatory viewing for . . . well, everyone with a pulse.

It boggles the mind.

---

1 This despite the fact that I'm an incredibly picky eater and a reasonably picky everything-elser, so trust me when I say that if *you* like something, chances are I don't.

But of all the demographic groups who foolishly insisted on ignoring this show (and alas, they are legion), the one that has always puzzled me the most are the teenagers. After all, *Friday Night Lights* isn't just a show about teens—it's a show about breathtakingly beautiful teens, engaged in the full gamut of thrilling, scandalous, melodramatic, angst-filled teenage activities. The show was hailed by critics for its painfully real depictions of adolescence; it's got plenty of sex, drugs, and (inspired choices of) rock and roll; it's got torment and romance, state championships and cheerleading wars, keg parties and pregnancy scares; it's got—and you'd think this would be enough in itself—*Tim Riggins*.

Yet the show had no vocal teen following. It lasted less than two months in syndication on ABC Family (the teen-driven cable network currently home to *Pretty Little Liars*, *The Secret Life of the American Teenager*, and *Make It Or Break It*, a show that at least one reviewer somewhat abashedly deemed "the *Friday Night Lights* of women's gymnastics").[2] *Friday Night Lights* is an unapologetically teen show that somehow failed to appeal to a critical mass of teenagers. And, after much gnashing of teeth and wracking of brains, I finally figured out that this was by design. *Friday Night Lights* is a show *about* teenagers, yes. But, despite heaping helpings of soapy melodrama acted out by a plethora of *Tiger Beat*–worthy actors, it's not a show *for* teenagers.[3]

The question is: why not?

---

2 This was *Slate* TV critic Troy Patterson, who also noted that without anyone noticing, the channel has begun to air "teen shows that teens actually watch" (2009).

3 Just to be clear: I'm by no means saying that *no* teens watched *Friday Night Lights*, or that no teens should. (When I say everyone on the planet should be watching this show, I mean *everyone*.) Obviously plenty of teenagers like stuff that isn't designed especially for them, just as plenty of adults, no matter how abashedly, like stuff that is.

A Brief (and Hopefully Unnecessary) Message from Your Sponsor

If you haven't watched a teen show since *Saved By the Bell* or *The Partridge Family*, you can be excused for (mistakenly) thinking this isn't a puzzle but a simple logical syllogism:[4]

> *Teen shows are crap.*
> Friday Night Lights *is not crap.*
> *Therefore,* Friday Night Lights *is not a teen show.*

I write for teens for a living, so maybe I'm a little biased when it comes to believing that stories crafted specifically for teenagers can be of just as high a quality as those designed for adults.

Biased or not, I'm also right. If I weren't, reviewers wouldn't expend quite so much saliva drooling over critical darlings like *My So-Called Life*, *Freaks and Geeks*, *Veronica Mars*, and *Buffy the Vampire Slayer*. There's no such thing as being "too good" to be a teen show, nor does brilliance have a repulsive effect on teen viewers.[5]

I would argue the issue lies not with *Friday Night Lights'* quality, but with its realism. *Friday Night Lights* shows us what being a teenager is like with painful accuracy—and this is its problem. Accuracy requires two things: objectivity and distance.

---

4 Personally, I feel that while *Saved By the Bell* may not offer the most aesthetically, dramatically, or intellectually sophisticated viewing experience, it nonetheless contains the answers to nearly all of life's most important questions. But that's an argument for another day.

5 Yes, there are some shows that offer us a dense, thorny tapestry of confusing themes and half-articulated emotions needing a lifetime of experience and study to even begin to comprehend. But *Friday Night Lights* isn't *The Wire*; it isn't *Carnivale*; it isn't even *The West Wing*. It's a plain-spoken, simply plotted, high-class melodrama—and that's why we love it.

And it's hard to be either objective about or distant from adolescence when you're still in the midst of it. While *Friday Night Lights* tells us what adolescence *is*, shows made for and speaking to people still trapped in the hell of their teen years tell us how adolescence *feels*. They sacrifice realism for emotional truth; they replace nostalgic distance with painful immediacy. They show us a world distorted by the funhouse mirror of the teen mind. It's a world very different than the world of Dillon, Texas, where adolescence is a state not of alienation and revolution but of integration and evolution, where The Man generally knows what he's talking about, where nothing changes and no one is ever alone.

You can almost understand why teen viewers searching for a reflection of their own lives might be tempted to change the channel.

Parents Just Don't Understand (Unless They Live in Dillon, Texas)

The most obvious of *Friday Night Lights'* teen repellents is the prevalence of adult characters—or, more to the point (since every teen show these days comes with its obligatory parental plotlines), the prevalence of adult characters with compelling and sympathetic points of view. Seeing parents having on-screen sex is bad enough—but seeing them as *real* people, with flaws, doubts, problems, strengths, loves, lusts, dreams, and fears as powerful as your own?[6] I don't know about you, but when I

---

6 *Gilmore Girls*, with its large adult cast and very present maternal figure, would at first seem to offer a strong counterexample. But structurally, *Gilmore Girls* was almost two shows in one: Rory and Lorelei moved through their plotlines and their worlds separately, and when their relationship did take center stage, it was generally because they were fighting. And in fairness,

was a teenager, this was a reality I was very much not prepared to handle.

Compare *Friday Night Lights'* omnipresent—and generally extremely-in-the-loop—grown-ups to the over-thirty brigade on a show like *The O.C.* or *Gossip Girl*, where adults are kept sequestered on their own side of the canvas, occasionally popping by to dole out wisdom or alcohol but more often leaving their feral teens to fend for themselves. Even on shows with a somewhat more wholesome interpretation of parenting (*Dawson's Creek*, *My So-Called Life*, the original *90210* in which the Walsh paterfamilias came straight out of the *Brady Bunch*), parents are as irrelevant as they are oblivious.[7]

Accuracy is sacrificed at the altar of emotional truth: most teens don't live in a world magically depopulated of adults. But if the most important things in your life are things that your parents have no part in (things your parents don't even know about or wouldn't allow if they did), it's easy for parents to seem irrelevant, and, no matter how many dinners they supply or groundings they issue, their irrelevance functionally equates to absence.

Not in Dillon, Texas. As Coach Taylor informed us in the pilot, warning his players of the shame and devastation that enemy teams would try to bring down on their heads, "They're gonna attempt to do this [tear you apart] in front of your mothers, in front of your fathers, in front of your brothers, in front of your sisters." In *Friday Night Lights* country, your family is *always* watching.

And—contrary to what teen culture has been preaching since time immemorial—we're to take this as a good thing. The

---

it's hard to quantify Lorelei as an adult, given that the show was premised on her ridiculously prolonged adolescence. It's no coincidence that her increasing maturity kept pace with the show's downward spiral.

7 Poor Buffy Summers' mother was plagued by an especially dire case of maternal blindness, and—aside from her frequent cameos as a roadblock to Buffy's world-saving efforts—only impacted her daughter's story by dying.

interference, meddling, and counsel of adult authority figures is actively desired by *Friday Night Lights'* characters. It's a rare teen *Friday Night Lights* plotline that isn't at least partially shaped by parental involvement, something the show clues us into in the opening scenes of the pilot. Nearly every character is introduced to us in the context of his or her parents (or lack thereof): We meet Jason as his parents watch over him from the football stands; Smash, shouting at an interviewer that his dead father is no one's business but his own; Julie, who at first doesn't even get a name of her own but is noted only as "the coach's daughter"; Lyla reveling in her picture-perfect family; Matt struggling to be the man of the house; motherless Tim lying drunk in his sad filth, his first words on the show a reminder to Billy that, "You're a brother, don't forget. Not a mother." The only main character who struts on-screen without any familial context is Tyra—and it should be no surprise that Tyra is the character who seems most often out of place on the show, at loose ends or saddled with the kind of awkwardly bad story lines you'd prefer to forget.

The biggest problem most of these characters have with their parents? Wanting *more* of them.[8] Think of Tim and his deadbeat father, Vince and his junkie mother, Matt Saracen and his runaway mother, absent father, and fading grandmother—one character after another longing for authority and discipline. In Dillon, parental abandonment doesn't pave the way for a *Gossip Girl*-esque Eden, but in fact has the opposite effect, forcing adult responsibilities onto characters who spend more time worrying

---

8 The exception here, of course, is Joe McCoy, a bad-daddy who seemed like he escaped from a Pat Conroy novel. But I'd argue that McCoy was the exception that proved the rule. On a show crammed with nuanced, three-dimensional, sympathetic portraits of even the most initially loathsome-seeming characters (I love you, Buddy Garrity), McCoy stuck out as a cardboard villain. The viewer waited patiently all through season three for him to get some kind of characterization beyond *asshole*, because this show is simply not in the habit of straightforward villains *or* actively bad parenting.

about cooking, cleaning, and paying the bills than they do about what to wear to the prom.

Of course, these characters don't have to worry too much, because Dillon, Texas, has a ready cure for Parental Abandonment Syndrome: Eric and Tami Taylor. If *My So-Called Life* and *Buffy*[9] and even *Saved By the Bell* call on the youth of America to rage against the machine, to distrust authority figures and speak truth to power, *Friday Night Lights* is here to counter that The Man is almost always right.

Especially when The Man is Coach Eric Taylor.

It's apparently not enough for Coach and Mrs. Coach to put all other parents, real and fictional, to shame. Over the run of the series they've served as surrogate parents to pretty much every character on the canvas (even including some of the adults). It's no coincidence that Coach Taylor calls his players "son." They are all his boys: his responsibility. And far from resenting him for overreaching or pushing too hard or poking his adorable nose where it doesn't belong, we worship him, as do the boys, for his determination to mold them into men.

Those who react to this meddling in more typical adolescent fashion, chafing against his will, don't last very long. New Orleans exile Voodoo Tatum's open defiance made him a pariah with the players and the viewers within seconds of his first appearance, and in the end it didn't matter whether his attitude had cause. (Voodoo's naked disgust for authority stands in stark contrast with Tim Riggins' instinctive respect for it. Though he begins the show as the classic drunken, temperamental bad boy, he's a bad boy who never fails to address adults as ma'am and sir.) Characters who have the audacity to challenge the coach are either a)

---

9 *Buffy* may have given us a beloved authority figure in Giles . . . but it also gave us an arrogant and incompetent Watchers' Council, a weasely principal in league with a demonic mayor, and the vicarious pleasure of watching another dictatorial principal get devoured by his own students.

like Voodoo, swiftly dispensed with, b) like J.D. McCoy, turned into villains, or c) like Smash and Tim, suitably chastened and repentant by episode's end.

In Dillon, Texas, resistance is futile.

On another show, this unquestioning obedience might be cast in a rather sinister light. But here there is no need for concern because we know Coach Taylor to be a benevolent dictator. This fantasy of the perfect father figure lies at the heart of the show—yes, we watch for Jason's inspirational struggle, Buddy's smarmy charm, Matt and Julie's love, Tim Riggins' cheekbones, but at the end of the day, we're *really* watching for those stirring speeches Coach delivers, challenging his sons to rise to greatness. We watch him boss them around, shout at them, berate them, advise them, shape them; we watch him, episode after episode, tell them what they should do; we watch them, one by one, fall into line.

We watch because it's the closest we can come to having a Coach Taylor of our own tell *us* what to do.

The More Things Change . . .

If the teen years are characterized by a rebellion against authority, they're consumed (some might say plagued) by a rebellion against the self. More specifically, a rebellion against the worn-out childhood self that no longer seems to suit, the unfamiliar and undesirable self in the mirror, studded with pimples and awkward curves and inconvenient hair, the false and ill-fitting self that's been imposed by those annoying authority figures, or by judgmental friends, or by a hostile world that refuses to see the real you.

Of course, if "the real me" were a self-evident concept, there would be far fewer emo songs and Hot Topics. As TV teaches us, adolescence is a time for trying on and casting off identities as if they were shoes. It's why we meet most of television's teen characters at a time of transformation: as their series open, Rory Gilmore is starting a new school, Lindsay Weir is ditching the Mathletes, Brenda Walsh and Buffy Summers are sampling a new zip code, and Angela Chase is choosing a new hair color that will be better suited to her new best friend. These are teens in metamorphosis—rejecting not just the past, but the self.

Not our friends in Dillon. Even if they wanted to renounce their identities, the town wouldn't let them. They may be realistic, three-dimensional characters, but they're also recognizable small-town archetypes: the town quarterback, the town good girl, the town drunk, the town skank. When one of these roles is renounced—which is less frequently than one might expect—it's only to trade it for an equally familiar one. Of course the characters develop and grow, but they don't transform into something unrecognizable. They don't dye their hair neon colors or ditch their old friends and old hobbies. There's no such thing as discontinuity with the past when you live in a place where you can't go to the grocery store without running into someone who knew you when you were still in diapers.

Successful *Friday Night Lights* plotlines about new(ish) identities are handled in one of two ways: either a character grows into a new archetype, adjusting himself to fit a familiar, communally preordained persona (think Matt learning to play QB1—on and off the field), or a character grows into the best version of him or herself.

The latter of these strategies is exemplified by Tim and Lyla, who both briefly experiment with radically new identities, only to see their efforts fail miserably, and in the end embrace their original roles—town son and daughter—with enthusiasm. By the end of her run on the show Lyla may be a stronger, deeper person than she once was, but she's still the same obstinately cheerful, determined Lyla Garrity, following the rules and doing what she's told. Tim Riggins similarly evolves into a better, more sober version of the Riggins we meet from the very beginning—his rallying cry has always and will always be "Texas forever."[10] Characters like Julie, Smash, Landry—in all their years of angst and catastrophe, there's only one serious kind of crisis none of them have faced: an identity crisis.

The obvious exceptions here are Tyra and Jason, whose character arcs are all about a rejection of old identities and a struggle to find new ones. And can it be a coincidence that these stories of transformation—Tyra's pursuit of college (and occasionally Landry), Jason's quad rugby travails and teen fatherhood—are some of the show's least successful? The further these characters venture from their original roles, the less they belong. When Matt grows past his QB1 days, his character suffers the same fate (while we, as the viewer, suffer through a tedious *now I shall be an artist* plotline). And this, of course, becomes his exit plotline. In Dillon, it seems, the only way to change—really, radically change—is to leave.

Which is why Tim Riggins' enduring presence (dictated as it might be by Taylor Kitsch's contract negotiations) makes so much sense. Riggins *is* Dillon, and in many ways, he *is Friday Night Lights*. He has grown, but not changed, and this is one of the fundamental lessons the show teaches us (a lesson that I'd imagine few teenagers want to hear, much less believe): the more things change, the more they stay the same. This is the torment of small towns, but, as the show reveals and Riggins proves, it's also their reward.

---

10 When, at the start of season four, Tim Riggins literally tossed college to the wind and returned to his hometown and his default mode, we can argue about whether the moment represents a triumph or a failure, but there can be no argument that the moment is true to Tim, a character who has never wanted to escape his own life and doesn't understand the impulse in others.

Don't Stand So Close to Me

There's a reason I keep harping on the expectations and judgments of the *town*, and that's because in many ways the town is our viewpoint character. We are, like Dillon, omniscient, omnipresent, and highly judgmental. We see all—and, in terms of appealing to a teenage audience, that's way too much.

When it comes to books, there's an easy way to draw a boundary (admittedly porous) between those written *for* teenagers and those written *about* teenagers: it's all in the voice. Books intended for teenagers tell their stories from *within* the teen protagonist's experience. They have a quality of immediacy that's lacking in books like *Prep* or *A Separate Peace*, in which the narrators look back on events from the comfort and wisdom of old(er) age.[11]

It's a distinction that's harder to draw in television, when the camera can make everything seem equally immediate and nostalgic distance is used as a framing device without much impact on the tone. (Despite its hokey narration from the future, *How I Met Your Mother* is as firmly planted in its thirtysomethings-in-New-York present as the *Wonder Years* was in its 1960s family turmoil.) But teen shows do effectively the same thing as teen novels: They put us inside their protagonists' heads. They show us life through the distorting lens of adolescence. *My So-Called Life* did so explicitly, with Angela's angst-ridden voice-overs; *Veronica Mars* used its voice-overs to, in part, ensure that despite all the adult characters and plotlines, the audience was seeing the world through Veronica's spycam. Voice-over or not, all

---

11 Certainly there are books that straddle this line, and if you really want to see a bunch of young adult writers all riled up, herd them into a group, throw in some adult lit fic writers for good measure, and ask them whether *Catcher in the Rye* is YA. Then sit back and watch the fistfights ensue.

teen shows have this same sense of immediacy, this same tunnel vision. (As discussed above, this is why adults tend to recede into irrelevance.[12]) *Friday Night Lights*, on the other hand, pans wide. We see the world from the teens' perspective—and from everyone else's.

We see Julie through her parents' eyes, and this is one of the reasons that her bratty season-two story lines were all so annoying—on another show, it wouldn't have been so tempting to sympathize with her perfect parents. (Consider how we cringed and squirmed right alongside *My So-Called Life*'s Angela every time her mother tried to ask about her day. We didn't want her to suck it up and act like a human being—we fully understood and shared her excruciating need to flee.)

Think of any *Friday Night Lights* teen plotline—then try to think of it in isolation from the parents and the town. It's an impossible task. When Smash dabbled with steroids, it became a problem for his mother and his coach, and we couldn't help siding with them, taking the long view of his life when he could see only the next play, the next game. When, in the first season, Lyla refused to accept how Jason's injury would alter the shape of their lives, we sympathized—but we didn't empathize, because *we* knew she was delusional. We saw the tragedy through her eyes, but also through everyone else's—Jason's, of course, but also Buddy's, also Coach's, also the nurses', also the ladies' at the pancake dinner.

Lyla, as a teenager should and must, sees the world as she wants it to be. But we watch through the many eyes of Dillon, and so see her world as it *is*.

For such an emotionally intimate show, it's surprising to realize

---

12 And again, I would argue that those teen shows that are more generous with their adult characters, giving them independent story lines and sympathetic POVs, are usually those that—like *Gilmore Girls or Life Unexpected*—are premised on said adult characters acting like teenagers.

how much of it we experience from the outside looking in. When it comes to shared, *communal* moments of triumph and pain, we cheer and mourn as if these are our victories and our pain. But when it comes to individual suffering and decision-making, the show likes to play coy, showing us isolated glimpses, as if we were a nosy neighbor watching through a mottled window. Far from being a narrative failing, this distance is often present at moments when the show is at its best. (Remember that brutal season-one breakup between Tim and Tyra? We might as well have been strangers, pulled over to the side of the road to eavesdrop on a private conversation, for all the privileged insight we got into what was going on in either of their heads. We felt *for* them, but what they themselves felt remains, brilliantly, a mystery.) *Friday Night Lights* allows its characters their privacy.

The exception to all this is Matt Saracen. In many ways, Matt is the most successful, if not the only, truly teen character on the show—counterintuitive as this may seem, given that he's also the one with the most adult responsibilities. But Matt's story lines often had a sense of immediacy that the others lacked. When he's deciding whether or not to sleep with Julie, how to deal with the disappearance of his irritating interim girlfriend, whether to go to college and leave his grandmother in a home, how to make his father love him—whenever he's doing *anything* that matters, we're right there with him, at his side, inside his head.

This is because when we're with him, we're the only ones. Matt is alone. Profoundly, terrifyingly—and in a way none of our other characters can quite understand—alone. There's no adult gaze on him, judging his actions, worrying about his future, telling us, the audience, how we're supposed to feel about his behavior.[13] The town itself is befuddled by him and his inability

---

13 Even the Coach, surrogate father to almost all his "boys," is usually confounded by Matt—and, more to the point, by Matt's relationship with

to fit neatly into the role (QB1) they've prescribed. Matt is on his own, which means we have no one to translate his life for us and tell us how to feel about it. We can only feel what Matt is feeling, which is, more often than not, raw pain and confusion and terror and exhilaration—in other words, Matt feels like a teenager, and when we're with him, so do we.

Every teen *feels* alone. But in the *Friday Night Lights* universe, Matt's the only one who actually is.

Me Against the World

Every teen feels alone.

It's stated like a universal truth for a reason. This is the fundamental axiom of adolescence, the basis of all good teen angst:

No one understands me.
No one loves me.
No one knows the real *me.*

Emotional isolation is at the crux of the teen experience, and fiction targeted toward teens acknowledges this reality, treating its teens as existing in island universes of their own. It's a fiction of narcissism, which makes sense, since adolescence—a period in which the most profound and pressing question is always some variation of *who am I?*—is a fundamentally narcissistic state.[14] You are your entire world.

---

his daughter, which throws a wrench into his molding-boys-into-men machine.

14 Just to clarify, I'm using the word narcissistic in its least pejorative sense. There's nothing wrong with spending a few years obsessing about who you are and where you fit in the world. In fact, some of us are *still* working on that one . . .

Think Angela Chase, think Dawson Leery, think both the Freaks and the Geeks, think even of Blair Waldorf in her lovely but lonely penthouse, think above all of Buffy Summers: "Into every generation a Slayer is born: *one girl in all the world." One* chosen one, and she stands alone. The overwhelming sense of isolation doesn't diminish the important friendships and romances on these shows—to the contrary, each relationship becomes a lifeline. It matters so much exactly because these characters are so close to the brink; if they weren't aware of their own profound loneliness, they wouldn't be so desperate to find and hold onto those few people who truly understand. Friendships have a different quality when you're a teenager; small slights can take on life or death import; quarrels and abandonments can seem like the end of the world. This is because when you're aware of the abyss, you know how important it is not to let go, lest you fall.

But there is no abyss in Dillon, Texas.

In Dillon, there is no such thing as being alone.

"This team has never been about one player, it's about all of us," Coach Taylor reminded us ("Eyes Wide Open," 1-2). He said *team*, but he might as well have said *show*. "We're gonna need every one of us. Not one man; every single one of us. *Together*." Above all, *Friday Night Lights* is a show about being part of a team, and, by extension, a community. The interfering families, the claustrophobic town, the overarching importance of the concept of "team," even the intrusive and inescapable commentary of Slammin' Sammy Meade—everything and everyone in Dillon is *connected*.

Not that our *Friday Night Lights* teens always realize this. I'm not trying to say that the characters don't sometimes *feel* alone in the world. Who could feel more alone than Jason in that hospital bed, or Julie once she realized Matt had left her behind? But we know better. We know that these characters aren't as alone as they feel. We're with Julie in her misery, but we're also with her mother, desperate to help, with Landry, suffering in silence down the hall; we're with Jason in that bed, painfully and heartbreakingly, but we're also with Coach, standing over him; we're with Lyla cheerleading by his side; we're with Riggins—himself feeling like the loneliest man in the world—crying as he watches that game tape over and over again. The characters may, at times, see a world where they have no one but themselves, but that's not the world we see on our screens, and *Friday Night Lights* is good enough to make us believe our eyes.[15]

When the show is at its worst, it's because—as happened unfortunately often in season two, with Julie's rebellion, the Taylors' long-distance marriage, and Tyra and Landry's Excellent Murder Adventure—characters are segregated in their own little bubbles, with story lines that bear no relationship or import to one another. This also explains why the show has had such trouble introducing new characters, specifically those who arrive from out of town and have no communal ties (Voodoo Tatum, Santiago, Carlotta). They're outsiders in Dillon and so we feel, instinctually, they're outsiders to our show. You'd think that the introduction of so many new characters at once, in season four, would have been exponentially more disastrous, but this actually went much more smoothly, as Vince, Jess, Luke, and Becky were already a part of Dillon. Though it took us some time to care about them, we eventually did, thanks in no small part to the fact that they were all members of the Dillon community from the start.

If the show is weakest when its characters flail about in

---

15 Again, as discussed above, poor Matt is the exception to this rule. Is there a more desolate moment than when Matt, after being asked whether it was his job to make sure his grandmother took her medicine, paused and then said, "Well, there's, there's really no one else around . . . " ("Wind Sprints," 1-3)?

isolation, it's at its breathtaking best when the characters are *together*. In those moments when they experience life's peaks and valleys as a community, as a unit, we're with them every step of the way.[16] Even after all these years, a chill still runs up my spine every time the team is asked, "Who are you?" and answers in a deafening roar, "*We are the PANTHERS!*" (Or Lions, as the case may sadly be.) Jason Street's tragedy isn't just his tragedy; it's the team's tragedy; it's the town's tragedy. And at the end of that first episode, we spent very little time with Jason in that hospital bed. It was the team and the town's grief that we witnessed, as every single character came *together* in the hospital, weeping on the shoulders of strangers, while Coach Taylor's voice-over reminded us that though *we* would be tested, *we* would always persevere. These are moments when communal identity supersedes all individual identity; these are moments of apotheosis.

It's a scary thing to feel alone in the world—scarier still to believe that feeling will last forever. But adolescence is like that, a frozen moment, one that threatens to stretch to the horizon and beyond it. You may *know* the future is out there—graduation, college, The Rest of Your Life—but that doesn't mean you believe it. When you're sixteen years old, *this* is what matters: The here. The now. The prison you're in, not the parole you may someday be lucky enough to get. But *Friday Night Lights* puts adolescence back on a continuum; it reminds us, without need of a cheesy Elton John song, of the circle of life. It reminds us that adolescence is a journey. That you're still the child you once were and are already the man you'll grow up to be.

This is, after all, Coach Taylor's mission, and the show's

---

16 This is, I think, one of the reasons we see so much praying on the show. Not because it's a show about religion, but because on *Friday Night Lights* praying is an expression of the communal *we*. When we see praying, it's usually en masse—in the locker room, on the field, in church—with hands linked and heads bowed in unison.

mission: turning boys into men (and girls into women, thank you very much, although the degree to which that gets put on the backburner could be the subject of an entirely different essay). The show reminds us, over and over again: no man is an island. But every teenager *is*. That's the divide between *Friday Night Lights* and "teen" shows—the same divide between what we understand *now* and what we knew, at the bottom of our hearts and the pit of our souls, *then*.

Then we thought that we were blundering in the dark, reaching blindly for someone's hand and grabbing tight, stumbling in circles, alone and afraid. There is no dark on *Friday Night Lights*. Adolescence is played out on the football field in every sense of the word. Dillon teens grow up under the spotlights of a night game, on a field full of allies and enemies, encouraged and berated and guided by their coaches, watched over by a stadium full of fans, many of whom were once down on that field themselves and know exactly how it felt, all of whom have a vested interest in the outcome.

And for the teens of Dillon, we know—as we never did know when we were teenagers ourselves—that outcome is never in doubt. After all, clear eyes, full heart—*can't* lose.

From *The Washington Post's*
Jen Chaney

WHY WE LOVE
. . . Billy and Mindy Riggins

Billy and Mindy Riggins were never supposed to inspire us.

Billy was the washed-up former high school football player who drank too much, the kind of guy who was always scraping for cash, would piss in a sink if a toilet wasn't available, and would steal copper wire or illegally sell spare car parts if the opportunities presented themselves. Mindy Riggins, formerly Collette, was a stripper, a young woman with a sassy mouth, an affection for booze as strong as Billy's, and no sense of regret about taking off her clothes in exchange for dollar bills in her waistband.

When Billy proposed to Mindy—humbling himself at the Seven Señoritas Cantina by getting down on one knee in front of the entire margarita-swilling crowd—they seemed like two people who kind of deserved each other. And not necessarily in a good way.

But Billy and Mindy, two people with an undeniable white-trash streak in them, eventually impressed us. Despite their tendency to be screwups—actually, Billy overcompensated for both of them in that department—they proved they had loving hearts, a strong commitment to family, and the same relatable insecurities about their future as any young couple. Whether they were raising their baby Stevie, taking in a forlorn Becky, or preparing to welcome twin "Riglettes" into the world, they also demonstrated that they shared a surprising trait: a sense of responsibility, a word that had new meaning for Billy after brother Tim took the rap and went to prison for turning good ol' Riggins' Rigs into a chop shop. Together, these two were greater than the sum of their parts.

Of course, that doesn't mean they totally avoided a little healthy, unabashed trashiness now and then. Actually, that's one of the things we love about Billy and Mindy Riggins: they were tacky but they made no apologies for it. Some other things we love about them:

- Billy Riggins knows a little something about etiquette. That's why he showed up to dinner at the Taylors' house with a little gift. No, not a bottle of wine—a box of steak knives. Obviously.
- Mindy Collette crafted very sweet wedding vows. They just happened to be wedding vows that quoted dialogue from *Finding Nemo*.
- Despite all his experience in construction, Billy still managed to staple his hand to a wall while remodeling Buddy Garrity's house.
- Mindy insisted that her bridal shower should be a classy afternoon tea. And it was a classy afternoon tea . . . where strippers with names like Kandy and Charm spiked their tea with whiskey and danced around with lingerie on their heads.
- In addition to his politeness, Billy Riggins had impeccable business sense. Example: he chose to open Riggins' Rigs because it was "either this or a Quiznos." He also had a strong business model for Riggins' Rigs: fix cars, drink beer.
- Mindy Collette was the first bride on television, that we know of, who dared to wear fake wings with her wedding dress.

- When Mindy and Billy had a baby boy, they gave their son (first name: Steven) the ultimate respectable middle name: Hannibal.
- As assistant coach of the East Dillon Lions, Billy Riggins understood the importance of teaching his players a war cry.
- *Mindy wore an actual pair of wings with her wedding dress.* We know we said that earlier, but it's the sort of detail that really bears repeating.
- When Mindy felt threatened by Becky Sproles' presence in the Riggins household, she used the perfect pop culture analogy to express her concern: "I read *Us* magazine—that nanny with Jon and Kate. Look what happened to them." She eventually embraced Becky and treated her like a sister. So take that, Gosselins.
- Billy may have willingly let Tim take the fall by going to prison. But there was never a doubt that Billy loved his baby brother, took great pride in him, and ultimately admired him as the kind of guy Billy hoped to become.

Tim Riggins didn't think it was a good idea for Billy to speak at his parole hearing. "How badly can he mess it up?" asked Tim's attorney. "You'd be surprised," Tim drily replied.

To be fair, Billy did totally screw up his speech during that hearing. What actually surprised us, though, was how hard he tried not to screw up before and after—and how much Billy and Mindy earned our respect during their arc on *Friday Night Lights*.

"She needs a role model," Mindy said after she saw how abusive Becky's father and stepmother were. "And I think, unfortunately in this circumstance, we happen to be the role models."

She was right, except that it wasn't unfortunate. It was completely fortunate: for Becky, for Tim and Mindy, and for us, as viewers, who got to watch these two pseudoadults turn into actual adults, albeit ones who still have their flaws.

Our last *Friday Night Lights* glimpse of Billy Riggins showed him side by side with his brother, as they built a house together on that big swath of Texas land Tim bought. We like to think that all of them—Billy, Mindy, Tim, maybe Tyra and their kids—might live there someday.

Of course, when we watched that final moment, we also couldn't help but think: the Riggins boys built that house together? Lord, let's hope that thing has some structural integrity.

Friday Night Lights, NBC, and DirecTV

How an Unlikely Partnership Saved a Great Show and Pointed the Way to the Future

PAUL LEVINSON

Friday Night Lights was on the verge of extinction, the compelling stories of its vibrant characters about to be cut off, far short of any natural conclusion. Such are the hazards of airing on traditional network television, which provides the biggest audiences and the biggest risks. But a new kind of television came to the rescue, a kind of television that could be counted highly successful with fewer viewers.

The course of network television, its evolution as a medium, never did run smooth.

Star Trek showed that syndication could compete with network television in presentation of rerun dramas in the 1970s and first-run shows in the 1980s. *The Sopranos* showed that cable TV could compete with and even surpass network and syndicated television early in the twenty-first century—in both audience numbers and critical acclaim. And the story of *Friday Night Lights* and its sojourn on two kinds of television has shown that a superb show on network television—in this case, NBC—struggling nonetheless to find a large audience, can extend its life via partnership with a form of television different from both broadcast and cable: satellite television or, more specifically, DirecTV. The lesson we can learn from the sharing of *Friday Night Lights*' presentation to the public holds keys to the path for the future survival of network television in our age of iPads and iPhones.

How It Started

Friday Night Lights was born in the hearth of media symbiosis—a television drama series premiering in 2006, based on a 2004 movie that was in turn adapted from the 1990 book by H.G. Bissinger, which was nonfiction at that. Transplantations of narratives from one medium to another—remakes—are no easy proposition or path to success. They are vulnerable to what I call "the first love syndrome," or our tendency to hold the first presentation of a story that we have come to love above all subsequent presentations, and as the standard against which we judge them.

By all accounts, however, including mine, *Friday Night Lights* on television was far better than the movie, which was mainly a story of high school football with minimal exposition of personal and family relationships (the book, being nonfiction, is not really comparable to the movie or the television show). Connie Britton, who plays the coach's wife in both presentations, provides a vivid example of the difference between the movie and television series. In the movie, she has a negligible part, with barely a line. In the television series, her portrayal of Tami Taylor brings us what I would say is the best portrayal of a wife ever on television. Peter Berg created both the movie and television series, but the length of the television drama—thirteen to twenty-two hours per season in the case of *Friday Night Lights* in comparison to just a single two-hour showing for the movie—allowed him to endow the television drama with levels of realistic narrative rarely seen on either the motion picture or television screen. *Friday Night Lights* on television was much more about life in a small Texas town than about football, and it managed to tell riveting stories without recourse to constant gunplay, medical crises, and other staples of network television.

The show was lionized by critics from the *New York Times*, the *Washington Post*, *Time*, and *TV Guide* (see the Wikipedia article on *Friday Night Lights* for a summary, which also includes references to the few critics who did not like the series). But the ratings were weak at the outset—rarely attracting more than 7 million viewers after the premiere—and only got worse. By the end of the second season of *Friday Night Lights* on NBC, with an audience of just a little over 5 million, the show that was the fully warranted darling of critics was headed for cancellation.

What Went Wrong at NBC?

Television audiences have fallen a long way since *Dallas* regularly attracted 50 million and more viewers on CBS in the 1980s. But *NCIS*, the most watched drama on television today, attracts 18 to 19 million viewers to CBS, and the big four traditional broadcast television networks (CBS, ABC, NBC, and Fox) like to see at least 10 million in the audience for a show to be judged as viable or worthy of continuation. Why did *Friday Night Lights* have trouble attracting even 6 million viewers on NBC?

All kinds of plausible explanations are possible. The series was at first pitched to the public as a football story, in hopes that it would attract enough male viewers—the predominant gender in football fandom—to make up for the relative paucity of female football fans. When that didn't work, NBC switched focus and began promoting the human relationships on the show in an attempt to attract more female viewers. The tagline "it's about life" became prominent in *Friday Night Lights'* promotion. But that didn't work, either.

NBC began offering every episode online in the first season, for free, on NBC.com in December 2006. NBC changed the day of the week *Friday Night Lights* was shown—from Wednesdays in season one to Fridays in season two—a good idea, since the title of the series suggests a Friday-night showing, even though Friday night is usually the graveyard slot—but the ratings still declined. Nothing seemed to help. And the writers' strike in 2007–2008, which disrupted the viewership of most of the shows on television that year, was especially damaging to a series already struggling to find and keep its audience in its second season.

So why, then, was such a good show such a tough sell? The answer likely resides in an irony: the very qualities that lifted *Friday Night Lights* above the pack made it less likely to attract droves of viewers. *Friday Night Lights* was indeed not a cop or a doctor show, or even a show about typically teenager soap opera issues. Nor was it a show about young adults with super powers, such as *Heroes,* which attracted an average of 14.3 million viewers per episode in its debut season on NBC, the same 2006–2007 season in which *Friday Night Lights* premiered. A story about real people with real problems—not how can I practice my super powers without my teachers or parents discovering that I'm somehow more than human—had an audience at best only half the size of the one watching people fly and walk through walls in *Heroes.*

But numbers are relative, especially when they apply to audiences for popular culture. Five to 7 million may have been puny to a traditional television network, accustomed to audiences as much as ten times that in its past and insistent on audiences at least twice the size of 5 million in the present, but 5 million and any higher numbers were considered pay dirt, the pot of gold at the end of the rainbow, by nontraditional network television such as cable.

The Sopranos on HBO, which I argued back in 2002 had broken the traditional network monopoly in attracting reliably large numbers of viewers, averaged 8 million viewers from its second season onward. AMC's *Mad Men*, critically acclaimed and award-winning like *The Sopranos*—and the product of Matthew Weiner, one of *The Sopranos'* prime creative forces later in the series—has averaged 2 to 3 million viewers in every season after its debut year. *The Closer*, also award-winning and applauded by the critics, has drawn 5 to 6 million viewers per episode in its six seasons on TNT—or almost exactly the numbers that were pulling *Friday Night Lights* down to extinction on NBC.

None of those highly successful shows are about everyday people. Suburban gangsters (*The Sopranos*), advertising execs and writers in the 1960s (*Mad Men*), and police detectives in Los Angeles (*The Closer*) have little in common with the lives of most Americans. But this show "about life" that generated the same size audiences as *The Closer* still had great appeal to a nonnetwork form of television—indeed, one that was accustomed to far smaller audiences for its original programming than even cable.

Enter DirecTV

DirecTV and its main competitor, the Dish Network, provide television via direct satellite broadcast or transmission. As such, DirecTV can be considered part of the third wave of television presentation, after traditional network television (which became a commercially successful mass medium in the 1940s, and of which NBC is an example) and cable television (which became a major television player in the early 1980s, and of which HBO, AMC, and TNT are examples).

Satellite television is not only the most recent part of the triad—DirecTV was launched in 1994, and the Dish Network in 1996—but is also the smallest, in terms of numbers of viewers. DirecTV has 18 million subscribers and Dish has 14 million, in contrast to HBO, for example, which has more than 28 million subscribers and is just one network of many on cable. And satellite television's position as the leading edge of television-presentation evolution was short-lived, quickly giving way to YouTube, iTunes, and various forms of television on the Web, and telephone-company (such as Verizon) delivery of television through fiber optics, both of which became prominent television players in the first decade of the twenty-first century.

The relationship between programming and delivery among these providers is complex and overlapping. NBC's content is carried on cable and satellite television. HBO's content is available on satellite, and DirecTV's original programming is delivered not just via satellite but on Verizon's fiber optic network. This mix makes it advisable for individual players such as DirecTV to do whatever they can to be more uniquely identifiable to the public. Original programming, or television shows available only on a given delivery system, is one way to accomplish this. But production of original television programming is expensive. Co-producing reduces this burden, as does acquiring "first-run" series from other networks (series not shown previously because the originating network decided not to air them). Both methods provide many of the benefits of totally original programming.

DirecTV began to offer original programming—concerts and various events—in 1999. By 2005, DirecTV's original offerings were situated on The 101 Network (previously called Freeview). *Supreme Court of Comedy* (an original spoof court show, with comedians and real plaintiffs and defendants) and *Rock in a Hard*

Place (an original game show in which celebrity rock bands are the contestants) both debuted on 101 in 2008. Original and semi-original programming were clearly in the air on DirecTV. NBC's soap opera *Passions* moved to DirecTV for its first-run presentation in 2007, where it lasted a year before being cancelled. The third season of NBC's *Friday Night Lights* debuted not on NBC, but on DirecTV's 101 in the fall of 2008, and did better than *Passions*.

Friday Night Lights on DirecTV

Friday Night Lights' audiences on NBC had dropped from between 6 and 7 million in the first season, to between 5 and 6 million in the second season, and then to around 4 or 5 million in its third season, which was the season that *Friday Night Lights* was presented first on DirecTV. The acquisition of *Friday Night Lights* by DirecTV can thus be seen as an inoculation that saved the life of the series—it certainly would not have been renewed on NBC, where, as we have seen, 5 million viewers is too low to sustain a series. Or, as NBC president Ben Silverman had told a reporter from *TV Squad* back in 2008: "I love it. You love it. Unfortunately, no one watches it."[1] In the cold arithmetic of traditional network television, 5 million viewers equals no one.

But from NBC's viewpoint, the sharing of *Friday Night Lights* with another network was a way to keep the series alive and amortize the big production investment they had already made in the show. NBC had previously made a similar move with its sharing of part of its *Law & Order* franchise and expenses with basic cable's USA Network (owned by NBC Universal, making such an arrangement easier), which began presenting first runs of *Law & Order:*

---

1 Bob Sassone, TV Squad, February 5, 2008.

Criminal Intent in its seventh season in 2007. Declining ratings on NBC had motivated the change, but *Criminal Intent* became the most-watched television series on basic cable (basic cable comes with most cable subscriptions at no additional cost, in contrast to premium cable networks such as HBO, which cost extra).

The third season of *Friday Night Lights* was also pivotal and crucial in its content, or how its story line progressed and reset the series. After a path-breaking first season that was unblinkingly and appealingly "about life," the series strayed a bit in the second season with stories about Jason Street seeking a miracle medical cure for his paralysis in Mexico, Lyla Garrity going off the deep end from football cheerleader to born-again fundamentalist teenage spokeswoman, and earnest Landry Clarke and his unlikely girlfriend Tyra Collette caught up in a murder. The other characters and their story arcs in the ensemble show—Tami and Eric Taylor, Tim Riggins, Matt Saracen, Smash Williams, and Julie Taylor—kept the series vibrant and grounded in reality, but it was due for a course correction in the third season, which it eminently received.

Friday Night Lights in its third season offered a full and satisfying plate of reflections of real life—struggles to get into college, make a buck, eke out and maintain some success and happiness in perpetually tough times. Its audience would not have been large enough for NBC to renew the series on its own. But it was big enough to get NBC and DirecTV to jointly renew the show for two more seasons, to be played first on DirecTV and then on NBC, just as had the third season. As Satellite TV Guru noted at the time—the end of March 2009—"NBC shares the production costs with DirecTV, DirecTV builds their reputation with original programming, and fans are happy to see their show continue. Everyone wins."[2]

---

2 Satellite TV Guru, "NBC and DirecTV Renew 'Friday Night Lights' For Two More Seasons", 2009.

The number of viewers that *Friday Night Lights* in fact attracted on DirecTV is instructive and shows the power that a much smaller audience can wield in a nontraditional television network environment. In contrast to the 5 to 6 million average number of viewers per episode that *Friday Night Lights* received in its second season on NBC, and the 4 to 5 million the series would receive for its third season on NBC (which would be the second showing of the third season), the premiere of the first showing of the third season of *Friday Night Lights* on DirecTV attracted an audience of just 400,000 viewers. Why was everyone—including NBC and DirecTV, which re-upped the series for another two seasons—cheering about such low viewership?

As the *New York Times* noted after the 400,000 audience was reported, that number "ranked No. 7 amid all of basic cable available to DirecTV viewers . . . Within the 18- to 49-year-old demographic, 'Friday Night Lights' ranked No. 2 with women and No. 7 with men."[3] In other words, DirecTV, whose programming was composed mostly of broadcast and cable television shows, was delighted that a show it coproduced, and was half or more its own, and unique in its first-run showing on all of television, was its seventh most popular show in comparison to its basic cable imports. Why was DirecTV so pleased about this? Because *Friday Night Lights* was a show that could not be seen in the fall of 2008 anyplace else, which provided at least one indisputable reason that a consumer should choose DirecTV over cable (and cable fiber optic), telephone fiber optic, or a rival satellite provider such as Dish. In this environment, a little audience could go a much longer way than in traditional network television.

The No. 2 ranking with female versus No. 7 with male viewers also was an indication that *Friday Night Lights* had

3 Brian Stelter, "A Small Satellite Audience for 'Friday Night Lights,'" *New York Times*, Oct. 7, 2008.

finally found its audience, one that was more than just football fans.

The Natural Lifespans of Television Shows

If I had to choose a single favorite line in the series—and there
are many memorable candidates—it would be from the second
season, when Riggins, driving along in his pickup truck, encountered Matt on the street, cutting school. Matt asked Riggins what
he was doing out of school. Riggins replied, matter-of-factly, "I
always skip Wednesdays." This is the kind of truthful, irresistible
snapshot of American high school life—an expression of what
every kid in high school surely wishes or wished he or she could
do (I certainly did)—that makes *Friday Night Lights* so original
and unusual. Its extraordinary quality, in other words, comes
from how clearly and vividly it presents thoughts, relationships,
and situations that are intrinsic to our ordinary lives.

But the series, as we have seen, certainly did not peak in
the second season, and indeed went on in the third season
and beyond to tell far better stories than in the second year.
More crucially, it went on to complete the stories it was already
telling. All narrative forms, including television shows, have
natural lifespans—meaning a point in which the reader, listener,
or viewer, regardless of the medium, will sense that the play
has run its course. Though this may vary depending upon the
commitment of the audience, the nature of the plot and the
characters generally will determine when that point might be
reached, if ever. *NCIS*, for example, could well run forever—
Gibbs (played by Mark Harmon) could be on the job solving
crimes against Naval personnel for years to come.

A story about a high school football team, even if it is also
and much more importantly about real life in a Texas town, can

enjoy no such security. Though the coach and his wife could continue with riveting narratives for years to come—with a focus on
grandchildren as well as on children—the same cannot be the
case for the football players and their girlfriends. Sure, new football players could be introduced as the original players went off
to college, car lots, offices in big cities, and maybe the pros, just
as Vince Howard and J.D. McCoy and others took over for Matt,
Smash, Tim, and Jason in *Friday Night Lights*. But however much
the audience might warm to the new characters, they would no
doubt still miss the unique chemistry of the original personalities,
which the audience had already come to love.

Friday Night Lights might have continued to tread water with
new major characters and gone on a few more seasons or longer.
Peter Berg could always try to bring back the series in a few years,
with mostly new characters except for Tami and Eric. But for
now, the extra two seasons made possible by NBC's collaboration with DirecTV allowed the series to resolve, if not finish, the
stories of most of the major original characters, who would have
likely moved on to other places in Texas and elsewhere even had
the series continued. Without those additional two years, the
show would have felt unfinished; with them, the show's cancellation feels less like a loss and more like a natural conclusion. Of all
the benefits network collaboration holds for viewers, this one—
its ability to allow stories that would otherwise be cut off too
soon to run their natural course—is perhaps the most rewarding.

Future Television Hybrids

The success of NBC's *Friday Night Lights* on DirecTV has already
borne fruit for another series. *Damages* stars Glenn Close as a
tough-as-nails, take-no-prisoners New York lawyer. It debuted
on the FX cable network in the summer of 2007. Like *Friday*

Night Lights, Damages received rave reviews. Unlike *Friday Night Lights, Damages* drew a record-breaking number of viewers the first night it aired—3.7 million—making it the most watched show on cable television. But *Damages* soon went the way of *Friday Night Lights* with an even more precipitously declining viewership, which dropped to under a million on its season-three finale in 2010. But DirecTV has picked up the fourth and fifth seasons of *Damages*, and beginning July 2011 the show will run there exclusively, with no FX repeats—thus going beyond the shared expenses and dual broadcast model of *Friday Night Lights*. DirecTV is clearly pleased with its *Friday Night Lights* experience—its VP for Entertainment and Production, Chris Long, told *Variety* that *Friday Night Lights* has "done unbelievably" for DirecTV (Weisman, 2010), while cautioning that his operation could "move away from that model" of programming in the future (which means, don't look to DirecTV to save every worthy show that fails to find an audience, such as *Lonestar* on Fox and *Rubicon* on AMC in the fall of 2010).[4]

And NBC is clearly happy about its part in that experience, too. *Southland*, a cop show, premiered on NBC in April 2009. A second season was in part produced and given a September 2009 premiere date on NBC. But the premiere was postponed and *Southland* was soon cancelled. Enter TNT on basic cable, which bought the show, aired the first two seasons, and in January 2011 began broadcasting a third season that it paid for in its entirety, with fewer episodes and a consequently smaller budget.

These kinds of hybrids, with shows exchanging partners like dancers in a Virginia reel, are a path for future success or at least the survival of television shows in a world in which television on our big screens at home is in increasing competition with what

---

4 Jon Weisnan, "DirecTV to curtail series-saving efforts," *Variety*, November 22, 2010.

the web offers to us on its smaller screens—including, also, television. Whether originating on network and going to satellite, or originating on cable and going to satellite, or vice versa, and with continuing partnerships or going it alone—whether the players are NBC and DirecTV, the FX network and DirecTV, NBC and TNT, or fill in the dance card with other choices—a significant part of television has become break-up, make-up, everything is shake-up, to paraphrase the Mamas and Papas song. Or, to switch metaphors to the political and the historical, the survival of television in the future may well reside in united we stand, divided we fall, with *Friday Night Lights* going down in history as the gleaming, pioneering touchdown in this new kind of partnership.

From *The Washington Post*'s
Jen Chaney

WHY WE LOVE

. . . Luke Cafferty

Luke Cafferty was a farm boy, the kind of guy who looked like he could appear in a Chevy truck commercial or perhaps inspire a patriotic adult-contemporary song by John Cougar Mellencamp.

His jawline was firm. His jeans were dusty. His belt buckles were large and oval-shaped. And as a kid who personified rock-solid American values, Luke could not have been more earnest and respectful, a habitual user of the words "sir" and "ma'am." This boy always wanted to do the right thing, even though, admittedly, he didn't always succeed. (Please refer to "pretending to live at a non-existent address" or "using under-the-table medication" for further information.)

Luke's mistakes were honest mistakes, missteps that didn't change the fact that, at his core, he was one of the good ones. He was forever loyal: to Becky Sproles, throughout her unplanned pregnancy and after the subsequent abortion; to Coach Taylor and the East Dillon Lions, despite that supposed offer to play for St. Pat's; to his teammates, even when some of them got offers from colleges that Luke desperately wanted to attend himself; and, as we ultimately learned, to his country.

That's why we love Luke Cafferty. We also love him because of the following:

- When Principal Tami Taylor caught Luke in his lie about which school district he lived in, he begged her not to remove him from the Dillon Panthers. Then, instead of pleading further or screaming at her, he did something unexpected: he apologized sincerely for not telling the truth.
- Most NFL players wouldn't injure a leg by getting it trapped in the fence of a cattle pen. Most NFL players wouldn't be able to mask their pain after such an incident, either. But hey, pro footballers aren't Luke Cafferty.
- Luke was willing to trade his beloved pig Mirabelle in order to make Becky his rally girl. Pig-trading = true love.
- Luke was responsible for uttering what was, perhaps, the sexiest pickup line in *Friday Night Lights* history not uttered by Tim Riggins: "I'm coming for you, Sproles," he promised Becky at the East Dillon luau. "Get ready. I'm coming for you."
- We love the fact that Luke was horrible at hip-hop and knew it, as demonstrated by his attempt to bust rhymes during a Lions road trip. "I like country, but this is rap/you put 'em together, it sounds like crap."
- After he took over as QB for Vince and won a big game, he found the confidence to bring Becky to dinner with his parents, the same people who quite publicly disapproved of Becky's decision to abort the baby. "Make the reservation for four," he boldly told his stunned mom and dad. It sounded almost, but not quite, as hot as "I'm coming for you, Sproles."

Luke Cafferty was wise enough to take the advice of veteran footballer Tim Riggins, who told the conflicted Lion that he should play in the state championship "like it's the last time you're ever going to lace up. Then, let it go."

And that's what Luke did, eventually placing his championship ring in the hand of his beloved Becky, boarding a bus, and leaving Dillon to join the military and fight for his country. We can't think of anyone we'd rather have on our nation's team.

From *The Washington Post's*
Jen Chaney

WHY WE LOVE
. . . Becky Sproles

When we first met Becky Sproles, all we could say about her was, "Oh, she's . . . cute." A seemingly vapid, stereotypical teenager with a fixation on winning beauty pageants, Becky initially came across as a Little Miss Sunshine. She also was the sort of girl who was manipulative enough to call Riggins' Rigs just to make Tim Riggins give her a ride. (In his tow truck, people. His tow truck.)

But over time, as we got to know her, we grew to love Becky Sproles. We adored the soft vulnerability in her eyes every time she looked longingly at the effortless hotness that is Tim Riggins. We appreciated that she maintained a strong relationship with her mother, even though the woman was constantly blowing her off. And we just flat-out admired the way she handled her unplanned pregnancy: how she immediately grasped the gravity of her situation, carefully weighed her options, and smartly sought counsel from the Oracle, otherwise known as Tami Taylor.

But most of all, we loved her relationship with Luke, which overcame its baggage then went on to exceed the *Friday Night Lights* season-five quota for cuteness. We also love Becky for these reasons:

- Becky could fill any potentially awkward silence with inane chatter. In fact, her ability to chatter incessantly about banal subjects—how her dog went missing, how her hair does a weird flip thing—was so strong one could almost call it a talent. Almost.

- Becky could say even more inane things before a committee of beauty pageant judges—"I hope that when I die, people will say that she gave more than she took. That would be true success to me"—and smile with such sweetness that she still won them over.
- Becky was smart enough to know that there was only one person qualified to help her find a beauty pageant gown with a portrait neckline. And that person was Tim Riggins.
- Ever the master of restraint, Becky called Tim at the wake for Matt Saracen's father. To her credit, she was polite enough to offer to hang up if Tim happened to be "near the dead guy."
- We completely understand why Becky had such a crush on Tim. We love the fact that her unabashed adoration compelled her to tell Tim that he's "not nothing." And we respect how she let go of those unrequited feelings while living with Billy and Mindy and became an honorary Riggins.
- After Luke Cafferty promised he was "coming for" Becky, she was wise enough to be there waiting for him—and to fall in love.

Of all the regular *Friday Night Lights* characters, Becky's final bow may have been the least satisfying. The last time we saw her, she was waving good-bye to Luke with tears in her eyes as he headed out of Dillon to join the military.

We don't like to think of Becky this way, as a mere weeping girl-friend, left behind and void of purpose. Becky Sproles proved that she was independent, capable of thinking for herself even when making the toughest of life's calls. So for Becky's sake, we hope that in the *Friday Night Lights* future we never saw, she stopped waiting tables at the Landing Strip. We hope she got a college education. And we hope that Luke came back to her, safe and well, so that the cattle rancher's son and the former beauty pageant hopeful could settle down on a farm of their own.

I loved that the postgame epilogue showed everyone at work: Vince practicing, Coach coaching, Luke enlisting, Tim building. In the land of [*Friday Night Lights*], work—hard work—brings satisfaction. I loved that [*Friday Night Lights*] allowed Tyra to blow off Tim, to recognize that they had different futures . . . I loved that State didn't really matter: Nothing that happened to any of the characters was changed by the game. The game didn't change their families, their jobs, their futures. The game, in the end, was just a game, and life flowed independent of it.

—**David Plotz**, "Series Finale: It Was Perfect,"
Slate.com

"It's Different for Girls"

SARAH MARIAN SELTZER

Friday Night Lights, with its focus on the dynamics around high school football, explores masculinity with nuance and humanism, showing the pitfalls faced by young men as they try to live up to social ideals of strength and dominance. But the show also delves into the pressures facing women in this man's world. *Friday Night Lights* has been lauded for its thoughtful, even groundbreaking, take on young women, particularly for an episode that featured a character choosing to have an abortion. This kind of praise is particularly rare in a bleak television environment where young women's sexuality—and women's sexuality in general—can be reduced to extremes: virgin or temptress, prude or sex object. On *Friday Night Lights*, the choice to see women as human and to acknowledge the social perils that make it "different for girls" is a bold one.

The struggles of *Friday Night Lights*' young women were most often seen through the eyes of Tami Taylor. Week after week, Coach Taylor endeavored to be a "molder of men." But Coach

Taylor's role wasn't unique. Beside him, Tami was a molder of women. Often laboring in her husband's shadow in their football-mad town, she strove to help mend the broken sexual and emotional lives of Dillon's young women. And in order to steer those women toward healthy choices, she had to steer herself away from echoing the widespread misogynist assumptions of her community. Tami's status as feminist icon for viewers (New York's NARAL chapter made "don't mess with Tami" T-shirts) doesn't come from an explicitly political or ideological stance she took—it would be strange to hear her call herself feminist or use words like "misogyny" or even "sexism." Instead, Tami's status comes from her own earned understanding that to help women, you cannot parrot degrading patriarchal language or assumptions. Whether she was comforting Lyla, who found herself in the position of school slut; navigating her daughter's burgeoning sexuality (which Tami desperately wanted to delay); or, ultimately, in the show's most explicitly feminist plot arc, sitting down to counsel a young woman seeking an abortion, Tami consistently chose empathy over being judgmental.

Similarly, through Tami's character, the writers of *Friday Night Lights* bravely replaced the conventional sexist stereotypes in television drama with a more honest attitude toward female sexuality. In Dillon, and on our TV screens, viewing women who make frowned-upon sexual choices as three-dimensional people, people who cannot be summed up by their sexuality, remains a radical decision, even if it shouldn't be. Through Tami Taylor, *Friday Night Lights'* writers embodied the courage it takes to treat young women with respect and dignity in a society that seeks to punish them for stepping down off a virtuous pedestal.

The Whore with the Website

In a seminal episode of the first season ("It's Different for Girls," 1-10), Lyla Garrity, formerly the quarterback's girlfriend and star cheerleader, arrived in her high school's hallways to find words like "slut" and "whore" sprayed on her locker. At cheerleading practice she slipped up and her teammates snickered in satisfaction. On the internet she found a "slam page," where she had been derided publicly. Sniveling boys approached her in the cafeteria, inviting her to a party in a taunting, lascivious way. All of these incidents represented Lyla's punishment from her peers after the school gossip mill got wind of her affair with Tim Riggins.

Tim was also punished for the illicit relationship but, as the episode title suggests, in ways that differed because of his gender. A group of boys took their aggression out on Tim's car, but once they did their damage, Tim was quickly allowed back into the pecking order as a football star. He had been adequately punished for his betrayal of Jason Street. Lyla, however, went on to face continual shunning and harassment for more than just cheating on Jason. Her vilification by a mob of classmates also resulted from her sexual behavior, which undermined gender expectations. A girl who sleeps with the quarterback and no one else is sexual in an acceptable way. Therefore, she had previously been "pure" as a female extension of Jason, the town hero. In deciding to sleep with Tim, she was making a choice that demonstrated her own sexual agency and personal fallibility—she was motivated by her own blatantly sexual desires and needs, not any man's. She transgressed the line between virginal and whore, embodying an "impure" sexuality that was deemed "slutty." In public, her entire identity became inverted. She went from the consummate good girl to the promiscuous pariah; her fall from grace was greeted with glee by the same students who had once revered her as the queen of wholesome propriety.

Lyla's treatment, and the episode's title, have deep meaning for the women of Dillon. The entire episode was framed around the double-standard theme, as Dillon gathered to see the cheerleaders compete in center stage, instead of in their squad's usual position buttressing the football team. As Jason, Tim, Tami, and the community watched the young women twirl and flip, *Friday Night Lights* showed us that women are under a different spotlight than men, both in Dillon's society and in ours. It's a harsher, less forgiving spotlight, governed by strict rules: if she makes one improper sexual move, the perky cheerleader grinning to applause today can become tomorrow's outcast and object of derision.

Lyla's plight was not just an object lesson for viewers, but a chance to show the characters' humanity, as well. Tami, Tim, and "bad girl" Tyra Collette—a woman who certainly knew what it's like to be reduced to her sexuality—all saw her sitting in the cafeteria, an object of shame. Tim chased the ogling boys away, but then Lyla begged him to leave, saying his presence just highlighted the reason for her shunning. "It's different for girls. You can sleep around all you want and people think you're cool," she said.

After Tim left Lyla's side, Tyra, despite being Lyla's rival, confronted him with the same complaint: he was making it worse for Lyla, and as a man he couldn't understand her position. And that night, in a parallel scene, Tami told Eric how upset she was by Lyla's ostracism: "It was medieval, you know. It was like *The Scarlet Letter* or something watching that girl walk across the cafeteria." Eric's glib response was that at least they were not burning women at the stake anymore. The fact that Lyla, Tyra, and Tami saw the same double standard that well-meaning men such as Tim and Eric missed highlights a shared understanding between women, the understanding that having everyone's eyes on you, having everyone see you as a slut, *feels* like being burned at the stake. As women operating in a sexist society, they know all too well that those leering eyes are not a chance occurrence, but part of a system that labels and demeans women based on their sexual behavior.

Tami didn't just empathize from a distance, but intervened in favor of sisterhood. She tried to pass on her own knowledge about coping with sexist harassment to Lyla when she later found Lyla staring at yet another anonymous smear note. "Well that's just bush league," said Tami. "We don't listen to those jackasses, come on." She put her arm around Lyla, led her through the halls, and then sat and took her hand as Lyla contemplated quitting cheerleading. Instead of telling Lyla what to do, she let Lyla vent her concerns, foreshadowing how she'd deal with other difficult choices young women would bring to her in subsequent story arcs. Unlike everyone else in town who had a prescription for Lyla's behavior, Tami chose to ask Lyla what *she* wanted and then supported those decisions. Tami's style of guidance was more feminist than anything else Lyla would find in a place like Dillon, or indeed than any female character would likely find on network TV.

The Sex Talk, Twice

Tami's patient ability to listen and not judge came easily with the students she encountered in her role as guidance counselor, but it was frequently put to the test when it came to her own daughter, Julie, younger and more sheltered than many of her peers at Dillon. While it took courage for Tami to help Lyla, it took far more effort to silence her own authoritative, even patriarchal, voice with Julie—her own offspring. While Tami easily took on the sexism others wielded against Lyla, she found it more difficult in a situation that was so emotionally loaded for her. She understandably wished to protect her daughter from the treatment Lyla had received. But to have a frank discussion with Julie without pushing her away, she had to silence that Puritan voice within *herself*. She had to live up to her personal principles that young women should be respected and that communication is more important than condemnation.

In another first-season episode ("I Think We Should Have Sex," 1-17), the Taylors tried to make sense of Julie's burgeoning (and very sweet) romance with Matt Saracen. Their bemusement reached a new level after a horrified Tami spied Matt purchasing condoms at the local pharmacy. From this sight sprang a sex talk between mother and daughter in which Tami confronted and then rejected her initial impulse to control her daughter's sexuality— even though her mother's instincts practically screamed that her daughter wasn't ready to be intimate.

Tami's first response to her daughter's sullen answers was authoritarian and conventional: "You are *not allowed* to have sex. You're *fifteen* years old." In angry tones, she was literally voicing the exact patriarchal standards that dogged Lyla and that Tami had previously combated: You are the good girl. You are my daughter. *You can't do this.* Furthermore, Tami's lost temper exemplified her less compassionate side, which was preventing her from doing what she wanted to do most: give Julie unqualified support.

During the course of the conversation, Tami calmed down, finally responding with phrases that indicated openness and a willingness to have a dialogue, rather than a reflection of social mores that prohibit teen sexuality:

TAMI: And I need you to be able to hear that. I need you to be able to hear me say that to you.

JULIE: I'm listening to you.

Tami struggled to replace reproach with guidance, finally telling her daughter, "*I want you to be able to talk to me about it*" —a far cry from her initial "you're not allowed." As she explained in a later conversation with Eric (who announced his own desire to send Julie to a "nunnery" and rip Matt Saracen's head off), she wanted Julie to be able to seek her counsel always, no matter what decisions she made—and Tami implicitly acknowledged that scolding Julie for being prematurely sexual, as the world likely would, wouldn't help.

Events favored Tami's assessment of her daughter's maturity— and her approach to handling their conversation. When Julie came home after *not* having sex with Matt, she succinctly thanked her mother for "the talk"—signaling that she had accepted Tami's input when it was couched in terms of woman-to-woman advice rather than hard and fast rules. Just as she earlier had done with Lyla, Tami helped Julie arrive at her own decision using warmth and support—but only after she realized she couldn't harangue Julie about her sexuality, even for her daughter's own good.

In order to empathize with a daughter whose sexual potential scared her, Tami had to look to her own experience. She admitted to Eric that she needed to improve on her relationship with her own mother, who offered only threats—which, Tami noted, did not have an effect. In this and other moments throughout the series, it was implied that Tami was a sexually active teenager. So just as she identified with Lyla as a young woman with a spotlight on her sexuality, she drew on her own experience of being threatened by her mother to find the right path for helping Julie.

Watching this episode, we felt immense sympathy for Julie both pressuring herself to lose her virginity, and then not being ready to live up to that pressure. But the show was no more or less sympathetic to the innocent Julie than to the sexually adventurous Tyra. Tyra may have made more aggressive sexual choices at Julie's age, but she also stood in a lingerie store with Julie and told her, with kindness in her voice, that she didn't have to have sex. Tyra was also espousing the view that sexuality shouldn't define a woman, but should instead be her free choice.

Tami's changed view of Tyra also ended up reflecting the show's sympathetic approach to this sexually sophisticated girl. Initially, Tami saw Tyra as a poor influence and forbade Julie from seeing her; later she apologized to Tyra and offered to help her explore her schoolwork as well as her social life. Again, Tami's better instincts to see Tyra as a person triumphed over her worse ones, which would have been to reduce Tyra to her sexuality, to see her as the community did: a girl headed for the strip joint after graduation.

Two years (and two seasons) later, Julie and Matt had broken up and gotten back together, while Tami had given a push to Tyra, who was now embarked on a bumpy journey toward college. In season three ("It Ain't Easy Being J.D. McCoy," 3-6), Eric and Tami were still fretting at the thought that Julie was mingling with the young men and women of Dillon, so many of whom had shown up at the Taylors' house, abandoned or in a jam. Eric and Tami respected those kids, but as their freak-out about Julie and Matt in season one demonstrated, deep down they wanted *their* daughter to be special: the happy product of a stable household. Although Tami had made progress when the specter of Julie's sexuality first reared its head, she hadn't excised all of her own internalization of society's judgmental attitudes toward teenage girls. Tami still didn't want her daughter to have sex, and she hadn't yet figured out why that was. She hadn't yet separated the strands of socially ingrained finger-wagging from the natural maternal protectiveness and strong nurturing instincts she felt toward her beloved Julie.

And so when Eric found their little girl in bed with Matt Saracen, in Matt's ramshackle house where so much drama and sadness had transpired, it was traumatic.

Nonetheless, the Taylors handled it much more calmly than they did the last time around. When Eric told his wife what he saw, Tami immediately stood up in her impatience to speak with their daughter.

"Wait. Before you go in there, you'd better know what you're going to say," Eric cautioned her. With shock written on her face—because of her usual ability to find a wise word—Tami realized that she had no clue. By waiting, Tami was able to access her hard-won feminist-minded philosophy instead of relying on her gut emotional reaction, which might have been to judge or berate her daughter.

Later in the episode, when Tami did broach the subject with Julie, Julie asked for her punishment in a glum voice—a reflection of the attitudes all around her, that sex (for girls) carries a penalty. But again, Tami's philosophy stepped in to counter this idea. "Your punishment is you have to have a talk with me," she said, a reflection of her own thought-out belief that conversation should preempt censure.

Tami asked Julie about love in her relationship, if they were using protection, and what kind. Julie said "condoms," bringing the conversation they had two seasons ago—prompted by Matt's condom purchase—full circle. This time, although she began with similar questions, Tami's soothing tone suggested anything other than the imposition of her own assumptions on her daughter. And even though Julie responded tersely, Tami gained the information she wanted in order to offer advice on physical safety. In fact, she was hell-bent on getting out the facts (facts that are great sex-ed for viewers, too) before they got into thornier emotional territory:

And you know, just 'cause you're having sex this one time doesn't mean that you have to all the time. And you know if it ever feels like he's taking you for granted, or you're not enjoying it you can stop anytime . . . and if you ever break up with Matt it's not like you have to have sex with the next boy necessarily.

And then the tears welled up in Tami's eyes, an emotional response. Tami, it seemed almost instinctively, counterbalanced that primal response by clarifying that Julie's action itself was not what prompted her sadness and that her tears were not punishment or intended to shame her daughter. She explained her feelings:

TAMI: . . . I wanted you to wait . . . but that's just because I want to protect you because I love you, and I want to make sure nothing bad ever happens to you. And I always want you to always be able to talk to me even if it's about something so hard like this.

JULIE: I didn't want to disappoint you.

[Tami shakes her head, hugs Julie.]

This time around, Tami used the "I want" construction rather than her previous and misguided "you are not allowed" to signal that her desires for her daughter to postpone sex came from *her own* protectiveness, her own maternal feelings, not some kind of absolute authority or conviction that sex is bad. She purposefully separated herself from the patriarchal standard that would have told Julie she was wrong for having sex—or more specifically that by "falling" into sex, she'd have to stay on that road and sleep with everyone else. *This is just me being a mom*, Tami explained, and *you are more than your sexuality*. She shook her head to make it clear that by having sex, Julie had not let her down in any way: her daughter's body, her daughter's choice.

Over the seasons, the show did a lovely job bookending these two sex talks. Like Tami, they saw Julie as a person, not someone defined by her sex life. The virginal Julie and the Julie sleeping with her boyfriend were written as the same character—and in fact, the sexually mature Julie was a stronger, softer, wiser person, not a fallen woman uglified or ruined by her sexuality. By showing us also how much of Tami's fear about her daughter's sexuality was entwined with her fear about her daughter growing up and her inability to protect her, the show gently demonstrated how much courage it took for Tami to let go—and what good parenting it was to do so.

The Hardest Choice

In many ways, Tami's effort at putting her internalized sexism aside and listening to her own daughter and the daughters of Dillon prepared her for her toughest counseling call. This occurred in season four ("I Can't," 4-10) when young Becky Sproles became pregnant after a one-night, virginity-losing stand with a new football star, Luke Cafferty. Tim Riggins, not knowing what else to do, brought Becky to the Taylors' door.

After Becky had spilled her dilemma, Tami carefully followed counseling protocol, ensuring that Becky was not endangered and urging her to talk with her mother—an echo of her own earlier concerns for Julie, her belief in open communication being paramount. She asked if Becky wanted referrals to teen parenting or adoption groups. Becky, though, was not sure she wanted to continue the pregnancy. Tami had an opportunity here to influence Becky's decision toward the one choice palatable to the community: accept the consequences (or punishment) for your actions. Have the baby. But instead, she did something that was radical for the world of Dillon: she merely smoothed away the surprise from her face and tried to be impartial.

And the show, like Tami, did something radical for the world of TV. It stepped back from the loaded politics of abortion to show us a young woman's decision. Becky did tell her mother, who flew into a rage—reminded of her own teen pregnancy—and they scheduled an abortion. Becky's mom didn't have the same perspective with her daughter that Tami did with Julie; younger, single, more vulnerable, her anger and disappointment could not be hidden. She didn't have a mate to talk over her response. She just had a desperate desire for her daughter's life to be better than hers. And her distress was further heightened by having to take two days off from work as a bartender and waitress due to a legally-required waiting period and a second doctor's visit before the abortion could take place.

The laws that delayed Becky's decision were put in place because of political pressure: to mandate that women "think twice" about a decision they've almost always already agonized over, and to erect hurdles in the way of the procedure. Most television shows make it seem easy to go to an actual abortion clinic, but in *Friday Night Lights* we not only saw the actual, realistic process, we saw it through the lens of Becky's fear and helplessness, a deeply personal perspective. Just showing Becky honestly—and not as a poster girl for sex's consequences—is a subversive choice. And once again, the show's view dovetailed with Tami's. She also saw Becky through the lens of human suffering when Becky returned seeking affirmation for her "weird" feelings. As Tami listened quietly to the girl's plea for understanding, her facial expression grew more sympathetic. Becky's poignant speech, which showed both how young she was and how much she'd weighed the decision, culminated in the most crucial exchange of the episode, in which Tami finally explicitly rejected the punishment paradigm:

BECKY: Do you think I am going to hell if I have an abortion?
TAMI: No, honey, I don't.

Here was yet another girl who thought that because of an act connected to her sexuality she deserved punishment—just as Lyla, Julie, and Tyra had in earlier seasons. Although Becky's projected regret was ostensibly because of the abortion, in the landscape of Becky's life, it was tied up with her first entrance into sexuality. It's not a huge leap to imagine that in the world of Dillon, girls who get abortions are considered "sluts" for the same reason Lyla was, because of its connotation of *sex without procreation*, or sex for its own sake. It also symbolizes female autonomy and agency, a woman taking control of her own body. That context is crucial to the lens through which *Friday Night Lights* views Becky's choice, and it's evident in Tami's response. Whatever Tami thought about the issue abstractly, should this pained, tortured young woman with so much life ahead of her really believe that she's facing damnation? Should she forever be haunted or labeled by a single sexual act and this wrenching choice? In an echo of how she softened watching Lyla and Tyra and her own daughter suffer, Tami's sympathy overwhelmed all other concerns, as Becky perhaps recognized:

BECKY: What would you tell your daughter?

TAMI: I would tell her to think about her life, think about what's important to her and what she wants, and I would tell her she's in a real tough spot and then I would support whatever decision she made.

BECKY: I can't take care of a baby. I can't.

Becky's decision was made—and it was her own decision, thanks to Tami's willingness to stand down. As she wanted to protect Julie and Lyla from the pain of adulthood, she chose to protect Becky by looking the girl in the eye and proclaiming her innocence, telling her she's not going to hell. Throughout the course of an hour, we watched Becky arrive there from an honest, nonideological standpoint.

But ideological controversy followed Tami in subsequent episodes—even as Becky, postabortion, returned to her teen existence. Luke's mother, an evangelical Christian, learned the story from Becky and instigated a campaign to fire Tami, who she claimed prodded Becky into her decision.

The irony in the political fallout was rich: Tami stood accused of forcing her values on Becky. But as we saw, she refused to do so, insisting on neutrality and support. Meanwhile, her enemies *did* have an agenda for young girls in town; they would have made Becky's choice for her. Again, merely treating Becky as a person with moral agency became a defiant act. But as Tami had learned through her interactions with her daughter, it was also the kindest and most effective way to offer advice.

With the calls for her head increasing, Tami faced a fork in the road with defending her integrity on one side, and saving her job and reputation on the other. Suddenly Becky's choice became Tami's; they were twinned, both decent women doing what they saw as the right thing when life threw them an impossible predicament. The writers were showing that all women, young and old, seasoned and inexperienced, face the same anger from a sexist society when they dare to make their own moral decisions regarding sexuality.

As Tami faced down an angry crowd, seeking to punish her by proxy for Becky's "immoral" behavior, viewers might have recalled Tami's own words four seasons earlier about Lyla: "It was medieval, you know. It was like *The Scarlet Letter* or something." Now she was the one who had to defend her empathy for her daughter and other young women who stood accused for their sexual choices. Back in season one, she told Lyla, "We don't listen to those jackasses, come on." She ended up taking her own advice, choosing to let go of her job rather than compromise her principles of respect for young women. By airing this plot arc despite a political climate that is particularly hostile to non-condemnatory depictions of abortion on television, *Friday Night Lights'* creators showed a similar resolve.

By the end of that season, Tami ultimately chose to go to East Dillon and to continue ministering to girls, to continue her mission to listen and not judge. Eventually, by the end of the series' run, Tami's mission was acknowledged and rewarded by Eric and by the show as being equally valid and important as being a winning football coach. Tami's struggle, doubtless familiar to many a female viewer or any viewer conscious of sexism, was shown with extraordinary depth throughout the five seasons of *Friday Night Lights*, a show that like its characters chose to resist sexist double standards and instead commit itself to the radical act of listening to girls' stories. By privileging the reality of those stories, and by privileging Tami's work alongside Eric's, *Friday Night Lights* showed us that a different narrative is possible—in girls' lives and in the art that chronicles them.

From *The Washington Post*'s
Jen Chaney

WHY WE LOVE
... Lyla Garrity

Lyla Garrity is a girl we should have hated. She was a cheerleader. She got straight A's at Dillon High. She's the epitome of the cute-meets-sexy female fantasy, the one every guy hopes to see naked in his bedroom as well as fully clothed, across the dinner table, when it's time to introduce the girlfriend to the parents.

Maybe that's why everyone at Dillon High was so unceasingly mean to her when word got out that she slept with Tim Riggins behind her paralyzed boyfriend Jason's back. They'd all been waiting for Little Miss Perfect to screw up, and when that day came, it was the equivalent of a very schadenfreude Christmas.

But here's the thing about Lyla: Yes, she's kind of a prissy pants. Yes, she grits her teeth too much when she's yelling at Tim for whatever absurd, thoughtless thing he's recently done. And yes, when she became a born-again Christian, she was so sweetly sanctimonious that you just wanted to push her pretty, ponytailed head in some holy water and hold it there for awhile.

But we still love her. Because underneath that seemingly flawless façade, she's got fortitude. She's got some fight in her. She's a good girl (the kind who dates nice Christian boys with preppy haircuts) with some definite bad girl in her (hence, Tim Riggins).

She can stand on the sidelines and cheer, but she also knows how to fire a gun. She prays hard, but also knows her way around a Playstation.

She can be there for Jason every single day he's in the hospital or rehab, even when his catheter isn't working and he can't feed himself. She can tell her philandering father where to get off but also, eventually, forgive him. And she can even turn the debauched Tim Riggins into a regular Sunday churchgoer . . . at least for a little while.

By the time she finished with Dillon, Texas, Lyla Garrity had learned how to dislike the sin but love the sinner, whether that sinner is her dad, Tim Riggins, or herself. And for that, as well as the reasons below, we love Lyla Garrity.

- Lyla Garrity managed to transform the polyester, chest-flattening Panthers cheerleading uniform—complete with turtleneck and hair bow—into the perfect ensemble for the Princess of Perky and Extreme Prettiness.
- When the relentless abuse about the Riggins affair—both at school and online—made Lyla quit the cheerleading squad, she reconsidered, showed up at the competition, and insisted on being signed in. "Yes," she confirmed, "I'm the whore with the website."
- Lyla may be a goody-goody. But she's still the kind of girlfriend who eagerly showed up at Jason's house with "dirty dirty quad porn."
- Hell had no fury like a Lyla when she was disappointed in her father and decided to wreck all the vehicles in his car dealership lot, then drive a car through his front window. Weirdly, this psychotic episode never came up in subsequent conversation.
- When Lyla needs to blow off some steam, she's not opposed to shooting at soda cans with a rifle. "Beats the hell out of making Rice Krispie treats." Amen, sister.

- When it comes to smart, quick-witted banter, Lyla Garrity can give as good as she gets. Example: when Tim Riggins chided Lyla by telling her to "Enjoy Jesus," she fired right back with a "Enjoy your depraved hedonism."
- When she moved in with the Riggins boys, she not only thrived in their messy, irresponsible atmosphere, she even outpartied No. 33 himself, adding insult to injury by referring to him as "grandpa."
- She once willingly rode a mechanical bull. If this had been promoted more effectively, *Friday Night Lights* undoubtedly would have seen a spike in (at least) male viewership.
- No matter how much she loved Tim, she was smart enough to know that if she had the chance to go to Vanderbilt and become her own woman, she had to take it.

Lyla Garrity was the only woman capable of breaking Tim Riggins' heart. She was the heartbreaker's heartbreaker. And thanks to him, she became a smart, responsible, very Christian girl who also has her eyes wide open to the joys of living life minute-to-minute. Occasionally, even with a beer in her hand.

WHY WE LOVE
. . . Tami Taylor

Working mothers are often told that it's not possible to have it all, or at least not at the same time. A mom can't simultaneously raise great kids, be a loving partner to her spouse, and excel in her chosen field—not unless she's some sort of superwoman.

Meet Superwoman. Her name is Tami Taylor, and every week on *Friday Night Lights* she conducted a master class in "I don't know how she does it," supporting her husband, Eric, at every football game, staying on top of daughter Julie's whereabouts (a full-time job by itself), and acting as the school guidance counselor (and, for a while, principal) determined to make each student realize every itty bitty ounce of his or her potential.

Sure, sometimes the whereabouts of her younger daughter, Gracie Belle, were decidedly unclear. (Was she at day care? With an unseen army of babysitters?) And sometimes Tami's behavior fell far short of perfect, as it did when she slapped Julie across the face after dragging her out of The Swede's front seat, or that time she threatened to have hottie English teacher Noah Barnett fired because of his allegedly inappropriate friendship with Julie. (To be fair regarding the former incident, we can kind of understand why a hormonal, postpartum Tami lost it a little. Like you wouldn't do the same if your impudent daughter stayed out past 2:00 a.m., then had the audacity to make out in front of your house with an older guy known for being Swedish, even though he clearly wasn't.)

But on most days, Tami Taylor was a self-actualized woman en fuego, effortlessly achieving work-life balance and earning the admiration of her colleagues and loved ones, all while looking hotter than Texas asphalt in her aviator sunglasses.

Despite her commitment to education and the benefits of the football lifestyle, how many times did it seem like the entire town of Dillon had turned against this woman? At least three: during the Jumbotron debacle, the flap over her removal of Luke Cafferty from Dillon High, and the controversy generated by Becky's abortion. Yet she persevered through all of it and came out on the other side smiling and well respected, aided always by her strength of character, her cool head, and a few glasses of wine.

Tami was more than a survivor, though. She was someone who helped other people overcome their obstacles. She loaned her persuasive charms to husband Eric Taylor so he could convince Jamarcus Hall's parents to let the boy play football. She convinced Tyra Collette to apply herself so she could get into a decent college. She recommended the plucky Jess Merriweather for the job of Panthers equipment manager. She even helped a distraught Matt Saracen arrange his father's funeral and saved him a few thousand dollars in the process.

Granted, she didn't always succeed in her attempts to straighten out the lives of others. Her effort to set the belligerent, troubled Epyck on the right path, for example, ended abruptly with a bump on Tami's head and the feisty Epyck headed for another foster home. But over and over again, when others willingly walked away from difficult situations, Tami tried. There is nothing but try in that woman.

Not only that, but she knew the right thing to say, almost without fail, in every situation—even when that situation involved talking to her eye-rolling daughter about sexual intercourse.

So forget all that new-agey advice you've received from Oprah Winfrey or Deepak Chopra. We prefer to live a life based on the principles of Tami Taylor, the mother, wife, and educator every woman aspires to be, as well as a character that we not only absolutely love but—okay, fine—kind of idolize. We learned enough lessons from Tami over five seasons of *Friday Night Lights* to easily fill an entire book, if not several volumes. So instead of merely recounting all the reasons we adore her, we've compiled this list of just a few of the Tami teaching moments we found most valuable.

- If you tell your husband you've gotten a job as a guidance counselor at the same high school where he works, he may respond by asking, "My school?" Answer with a combination of sarcasm and honesty: "I wasn't aware that you had bought it, but yeah, at the high school."

- Always remember that every conversation, even the most confrontational, goes much more smoothly with a well-placed "y'all."

- When your husband says he's uncomfortable with the notion of his wife working for an openly gay political candidate, there is only one proper way to respond: "Well, I guess you're going to have to be uncomfortable with it then."

- Never let your husband forget how much faith you have in him. Tell him things like, "I believe in you. I believe in you with every cell in my being." Assure him that playing a crucial football game in a cow pasture makes total sense. Stand by him through all his agonizing over which QB to start and his obsessive need to watch game tape. In return, he will show you that same unconditional love, especially at crucial moments, like when it's time to tell him you're pregnant the night before the state championship game.

- Drink a glass of wine after a hard day. Actually, you know what? Have two.

- Let's say you spot your daughter's boyfriend buying a box of condoms. Take the following steps: Tell your daughter you'd like to have a conversation about her possible sexual activity. Scream at her when she smirks at the term "make love." Insist that she's too young to have sex and would be wiser to wait. Then let her know that she can always talk to her mom about this sensitive subject because a girl is entitled to that with her mother. It's the best way to handle the situation, even though she'll still wind up having sex with Matt Saracen two seasons later and your husband will totally walk in on the two of them in bed together.

- If Glenn Reed, the counselor handling your maternity leave workload, suggests that perhaps you aren't taking proper care of your newborn, make sure he knows he's over-stepped his bounds. Also point out to Glenn that this isn't your "first barbecue."

- If your husband drinks too much and gets into a fistfight with your crazy-wealthy ex-boyfriend Mo MacArnold, make sure to talk AS LOUDLY AS POSSIBLE the next day while he recovers from his bruises and his hangover.

- When a pushy booster named Buddy Garrity ambushes you into spending precious school funds on an unnecessary Jumbotron, ambush him right back by publicly announcing that he plans to host a PTA silent auction at his car dealer-ship, even though he doesn't know it yet.

- Keep in mind that one's career does not have to follow the standard path, or even basic principles of logic. A person really can make the leap from guidance counselor to high school principal, then slide back down to head guidance counselor at a less celebrated high school, then vault straight to dean of admissions at a semiprestigious university.

- When the entire town is furious at you for making one of the best Dillon Panther players leave the team so he can earn his high school degree in the proper school district, do what makes total common sense: pull the car over and buy some chocolate.

- Do not get rattled when a jackass named Joe McCoy threatens to undo every Dillon Panther championship unless you allow Luke Cafferty to remain at Dillon. Instead, very calmly interrupt Joe's booster club luncheon and repeat his threats calmly, within earshot of many of the good ol' boys who might lose their championship rings if Joe makes good on his dastardly promises. Then sweetly say good-bye and breeze out of the restaurant with your head held high, knowing that you just schooled that smug bastard's ass. As always, don't forget to say y'all.

- As a mother, when your daughter disobeys your orders by going to Austin, it's your duty to leave her angry voice mails, harass Landry Clarke about her whereabouts, and fully prepare to punish her when she finally walks back through the front door. As a mother with a heart, it's also your duty to forget about all of this when she enters the house crying.

- If a young pregnant girl seeks your counsel, and every single thing you say to that girl is the right thing to tell a pregnant teen, do not apologize just to appease the school board and some irate pro-lifers. Instead, when it's time to speak at that press conference, say this: "I've always put the welfare of the students ahead of everything else. Every action that I made was with that intent. And it always will be. And that's all I have to say."

- Even though you love and respect your spouse, you still have the right to point out that he hasn't shown the grace to congratulate you on a spectacular job offer.

When we last saw Tami Taylor on *Friday Night Lights*, she was living in Philadelphia, a city whose residents may be less likely to appreciate her frequent use of the word y'all. Still, she looked elated and right at home on the campus of Braemore College, a place that bears a passing resemblance to the Boston university she once so happily visited with Julie.

Tami is in her element there, in a job she earned by demonstrating an unwavering commitment to her values as an educator. She's a sister who did it for herself.

But she's also a wife standing by her man, as we saw when she returned one more time to the football field to pick up husband Eric and take him home: home to their new life, in a new city, with their Gracie Belle. (Seriously, who's watching her again?)

We still don't know how Tami Taylor does it. But we know this: we love her like hell for making us believe that it can be done.

Friday Night Lights has always been the story of a football team and its coach, but it's also been the story of a marriage—one of the most well-rounded, admirable, memorable marriages ever portrayed on television. Time after time, this show's depiction of Eric and Tami Taylor's relationship has revealed the "happily married couples are boring" theory of dramatic writing for the ridiculous, lazy lie that it is. *This* happily married couple has never been boring, and they've been as much a part of the show's core as the Panthers or Lions.

> —**Alan Sepinwall**, "Series finale review: 'Friday Night Lights'—
> 'Always': Texas Forever?", What's Alan Watching on HitFix.com

[*Friday Night Lights*] managed to capture the many dichotomous moments in the life of a marriage. Where other TV series tend to focus either on the bickering or the saccharine, *Friday Night Lights* has thrived on nuance, creating domestic moments that simultaneously reflect adoration and frustration; tenderness and sarcasm; respect and fatigue.

> —**Maria Elena Fernandez**, "A 'Friday Night Lights' marriage
> that binds in many ways," LATimes.com

We tried to approach the stories with [Tami and Eric] in a way that would be real conflict—real things that would come up. And I do believe that within a marriage and within a good marriage, there are always challenges to that. There are always conflicts.

> —**Jason Katims**, interviewed by Alan Sepinwall, "Interview:
> Friday Night Lights' showrunner Jason Katims post-mortems
> the series finale," What's Alan Watching on HitFix.com

Sex, Lies, Booze, and the Perfect Marriage

What I Learned from Eric and Tami Taylor

JONNA RUBIN

Like most people who watch *Friday Night Lights*, I became desperate to convert new viewers. After all, we were constantly reminded by television critics that it was in perpetual grave danger of cancellation. If you're reading this, you probably share my sentiment that the show was too good to be in any danger, and perhaps you, like me, were wondering desperately what's wrong with American television viewers that shows like *Teen Mom* continue in perpetuity while Taylor Kitsch and his alter ego, the delectable Tim Riggins, toil in relative obscurity.

The problem, of course, came when I tried to explain what it was about. *Friday Night Lights* is hard to describe—is it about football? Uh, not really. Lord knows, I'm no football fan, yet I all but organized a write-in campaign to ensure the show's safety, year after year. Conversely, my husband insists it's the football that makes the show, and its emotional underpinnings, palatable for someone like him—the kind of person who would rather gnaw off his own fingers than endure another Mer-Der dramafest in *Grey's Anatomy.*

Yet, I will argue—and have argued, after more consideration than is probably healthy—that the very foundation of *Friday Night Lights* is as emotionally evocative as it gets, and its heart is *anything* but football. It is, of all things, the marriage of Eric and Tami Taylor. Without them—and their relationship—*Friday Night Lights* is little more than a house of cards festooned with cute photos of football players.

The cast of students, parents, and ancillary characters are a revolving door of attractive newcomers, with few exceptions. Minor characters become major players (I'm looking at you, Mindy Riggins), and characters who were once central to the plot of an entire season are relegated to mere passing mentions (Smash Williams) or the occasional guest star (Jason Street). And yet, the show goes on with nary a blip so long as Eric and Tami Taylor, the center of *Friday Night Lights*' solar system, continue to shine.

Not since, well, perhaps ever, has a couple captured the image of an enviably good marriage in a way that is so touching, realistic, and eminently watchable. The Taylors manage to take the ball-and-chain stereotype perpetuated by characters like Al and Peggy Bundy and the unrealistically romantic expectations of *The Bachelor* and turn them both directly on their heads.

It's easily the most authentic portrayal of a real, happy marriage, warts and all, but it also pulls off a feat that few long-term relationships, real or fictional, have done: it's still sexy. In fact, it's downright *hot.*

Throughout the five seasons of *Friday Night Lights*, though the Taylors' marriage rocks—sometimes hard, harder than many relationships could survive—the boat never tips over, much less sinks. It's remarkable to watch, really, and as a married woman, I am eerily fascinated. Why is it that their relationship works so well? Sure they communicate well, treat each other with respect, and all the other things we're taught make for a solid relationship, but it's got to be more than that, right? In fact, anyone who's been married, and plenty who haven't, knows that most advice is full of little more than useless platitudes that don't hold up under any sort of real marital discord. Marriage is, well, messy. Beautiful at its best; downright hideous at its worst. We see the Taylors experience both—surely there must be something we can learn from their marriage.

But while the Taylors do manage to sail through even the choppiest of marital waters with grace (well, mostly . . .), it's impossible to learn anything without understanding what makes their particular journey so rough in the first place. So before we look at how they make it work, let's talk a little bit about the challenges they're up against.

The Root of All Evil is Sleeping with the Boss . . . Sort of

Unlike many of their prime-time contemporaries, the Taylors are never threatened by infidelity or deep betrayal, and that's precisely what makes it so real to viewers. Let's face it, most people aren't living in an episode of *Dallas*, and most marriages are not tested by a sexy interloper, but by a partner's refusal to balance the checkbook or pick up his socks.

While there's no doubt that the Taylors endure a barrage of difficulties simply brought on by the burden of navigating life tethered to another person, not to mention parenting two daughters—one of whom is an unruly teenager whose antics would send anyone to a mental institution—few decisions have had a greater impact on their relationship than Tami's decision to join Eric at his place of business.

It's hard to believe that when we first met Tami and Eric, Tami was unemployed, apparently coming off of a fifteen-year stint as a stay-at-home mom. No one knows for sure what their dynamic was before they both had careers at (West, then East) Dillon High, but by the end of the series, her career defines her (and by extension, their marriage) as much as Eric's does him. It's tremendously ironic that in the second episode, Tami announced to Eric that it was time for her to get a job, but that it "ain't nothing for you to worry about" ("Eyes Wide Open," 1-2).

Oh, Tami. It's something for everyone to worry about. Especially because the job she ended up getting—without, it seems, much discussion—happened to be at Dillon High School, Eric's place of employment, where he had finally ascended to the closest thing Dillon has to a king. Or, as he put it, "his" high school, to which Tami sassily replied, "Well, I wasn't aware that you had bought it, but yeah . . . "

Look, I realize Dillon isn't a big place, and Tami, returning to the workforce after years of being a stay-at-home mom, was not likely to be in a position to be picky, but at a certain point she should have realized that this shouldn't have been a unilateral decision. Working together changed their entire relationship, and though they eventually regained their footing, it was not without cost. (Surely there were jobs in Larrabee?)

Tami already wielded influence over their home life—a role they both seemed comfortable with. But as Tami's career took off, in her position as guidance counselor and, later, principal, she began to have power over Eric's professional life as well. At first, it was subtle, and even beneficial—insisting, for example, that Tim Riggins get his academic career in hand before he could continue playing football. As Tami put it, letting Tim go through life stupid is bad for the world. (I don't care if he can't so much as spell "cat," so long as his biceps are in perfect condition, but who am I to argue with Tami Taylor?)

In fact, while Tami was guidance counselor, she and Eric maintained a relatively serene working relationship. It is only when she became principal, and thus his *de facto* boss, that things got out of control. It started relatively small, if by "small" you mean a very large Jumbotron. Taking on the boosters' Jumbotron initiative might have been the right thing to do for the students, but it pitted Tami directly against the people who are responsible for her husband's professional comfort. Worse, it left Eric, torn between his job and wife, entirely impotent as the foundation of both his job security and his family life began to erode.

Part of what makes infidelity such a threat—apart from the obvious—is that it provides another person with a measure of control over your marriage. And while Tami hardly strayed from Eric's side, she unwittingly handed the keys to their relationship over to other people the moment she became principal of Dillon High School. Worse, those people were the likes of Joe McCoy, and really, Joe McCoy shouldn't have the keys to anything, not even your grandmother's ancient Chevy Malibu.

Before long, McCoy, the boosters, and, it seemed, even the players were pitting Taylor against Taylor, ultimately leading Tami to play a role in ousting Eric as head coach, leaving him as little more than an outcast refugee in a bad part of town. No one likes to be caught up in a mess like that. But this wasn't some random employee she had a friendly working relationship with . . . this was her own *husband*.

(Side note: I'm not sure if this would have been viewed as egregiously, or even as noteworthy, had the roles—and sexes— somehow been reversed. But that's an issue we could explore for days. Years, even.)

As their foundation continued to sink, I couldn't help but think of another reason why this whole mess was so devastating, and it's purely superficial. A big part of why Eric is so attractive is his ability to remain, in many ways, the stereotypical male, at least at the "office." Aloofness, a tough exterior, and a certain degree of power are very attractive qualities. Look, maybe I've bought into one too many Gillette commercials, and maybe after this essay, a team of feminists (I'm thinking Gloria Steinem, Naomi Wolf, and even Betty Friedan, from beyond the grave) will stage an intervention, but I am completely smitten by a man who commands a remarkable amount of power, particularly over other men.

I mean, let's all be honest for a moment: at literal face value, John F. Kennedy and Bill Clinton were/are passably attractive at best. Throw the mantle of leader of the free world atop their heads, though, and everyone from legislative interns to Marilyn Monroe takes notice and considers taking off their pants.

I'm not pretending that Eric Taylor is anything close to presidential here, but if you manage to watch him manhandle a bunch of unruly (and delightfully sweaty) teenage boys, terrifying them into shouting "Sorry, sir!" if they so much as *breathe* incorrectly without getting a little hot and bothered, well, then, you should probably stop reading right now, because we have nothing to say to each other.

The result of all this is . . . well, it seemed like a collision course leading up to a spectacular train wreck, leaving their marriage as little more than collateral damage. The power shift was so pronounced and so abrupt that it could have easily left Eric feeling (and worse, appearing) impotent. Tami, despite her best efforts at embracing feminist ideals and becoming the poster child for having it all, found herself stuck with a husband whose virility was on the line, putting her attraction to him at risk. (This whole thing is like a cheese grater to Gloria Steinem's skin, and I'm so sorry, Gloria.)

Lesser marriages would have crashed and burned a long time ago. And yet, the Taylors come out the other side of each disaster not only intact, but stronger than ever. So how do they do it?

Rule #1: Get It On

Is sex the answer? Oh, hell, I don't know. I'm pretty sure Kim Cattrall (and her alter ego, Samantha Jones) thinks so, but for those of us who don't spend all of our free time considering whether the female orgasm is an art, we can at least consider whether there's something to be learned from Tami and Eric's sex life.

While we're (mercifully) never treated to the finer points of their lovemaking (it's a family show, people! Kind of . . .), we're left with the impression that they aren't exactly lacking in that area. It's obvious that they do it quite a bit, and if they don't, they at least keep things hot enough by suggestively teasing each other. Which, when you think about everything they've had to deal with, is no small feat. For God's sake, Tami all but takes a hatchet to Eric's manly bits, and yet, their sex life smolders on.

In "Eyes Wide Open" (1-2), she paid him a late-night visit at work, opening with a sexy kiss hello and the offer that "the field's empty, let's go make out!" And while he laughed, it was fairly obvious she wasn't kidding, or, at the very least, that they've had their fair share of illicit sex at the office (which, in Eric's case, includes a football field). For goodness' sake, they got into a full-on make-out session at the afterparty for Julie's dance recital that practically begged passersby to yell, "Get a room!" Still later, when scouting a potential home field after the town suffered a chemical spill, Eric took Tami to check it out, and within minutes, was rooting in the car for some blankets—which were most certainly not so they could stand up and watch the cows graze in the fading sunlight.

They have enough sex that it was a fairly significant issue in their relationship when they stopped after Tami gave birth to Gracie. Good gracious, the lengths Eric will go to get back in

Tami's pants! Things must be . . . impressive, I'm guessing, if he was willing to not only endure the world's most uncomfortable conversation with his assistant coach, Mac, about "getting back in the saddle," but he took every bit of Mac's advice, right down to the tulips he brought home. The fact that she rebuffed his initial efforts is almost moot, given the vigor with which they seemed to return to their old ways. Later in the season, Tami's confession to her sister Shelly that they were still struggling also felt insignificant and clearly baby-related. After all, they had had almost sixteen years of sexual bliss, unimpeded by the demands of small children and their unfortunate effects on the female anatomy after giving birth.

(Note: Perhaps the only unintentionally awkward moment in the series came when, in that same episode, after Tami talked about her book-club friends, Eric said, "You know what those people are? Those are bad, dirty people . . . " as he slinked toward her suggestively. I . . . what? Thinking about the book-club ladies being dirty people is supposed to be alluring? Oh, for God's sake, you might as well have worn a toupee and pretended to be Buddy Garrity, for all the fire that was going to light in her loins, Eric. No wonder you struck out that night! I kind of want to die thinking about it, if I'm being completely honest.)

Takeaway: Accost husband at his place of business more often. Make out at inappropriate places—perhaps daughter's preschool gatherings? Load car trunk with blankets.

Rule #2: Stay Well Lubricated

"Whatcha doin'?" Coach asked Tami in "After the Fall" (4-2).

"Drinkin' wine," she replied.

Color me surprised, Tami.

Frankly, I didn't notice this one at first—a good friend of mine pointed it out to me when I mentioned I had a thing for Tami Taylor. "Oh, is it because she always has wine?" she asked with a chuckle. Huh. I hadn't picked up on that, perhaps because I've been known to enjoy a nightly glass or two myself, and it's tough to observe our own habits, even in others. (This means I am clearly well on my way to becoming Tami Taylor. Perfect.)

Well, uh, it turns out she *does* always have wine. Always. Also, I suspect that Eric is not drinking Coke in those old-fashioned glasses he frequently carries. And he sure wasn't kicking back with a bottle of O'Doul's when he hit the bar with Buddy Garrity and, later, Virgil Merriweather. You don't forget where you parked your car when you're sucking down nothing but seltzer and lime. In fact, after rewatching the series from start to finish in a fairly short period of time, a good rule of thumb seems to be this: if Tami features prominently in the episode, wine will make an appearance.

In fact, wine (and, at least once, champagne) appears so often in the Taylors' relationship that it deserves its own line in the credits. Date night in a hotel? Order the champagne! Date night planned? "I got us our wine, and I need it! I need it right now!" said Tami. Get a bad article in the paper because you went toe-to-toe with the boosters over the Jumbotron? "I'll get more wine . . . " Eric immediately offered ("Tami Knows Best," 3-2).

What else are you going to do when your professional life is in shambles, in part because of your husband and/or wife, your teenage daughter is having sex with one of the football players and . . . well, let's just say I see why the Taylors drink so much. At a certain point, it becomes a necessary coping mechanism. And besides, how angry can you really get at your spouse when you're too blitzed to fully comprehend what they said in the first place?

Besides, there is always a bonus side effect in drunken make-up sex.

Takeaway: Well, at least this one is simple: drink more wine.

Rule #3: Lie . . . Sort Of

Part of what made the professional dynamic between Tami and Eric so strained, at least while she was principal, was that her new position of power clearly threw a cog in their well-oiled machine at home. With Eric the primary breadwinner, it wasn't surprising to learn that Tami ruled the home life with an iron fist, if in a velvet glove, and why not? Between practices, games, scrimmages, and an endless string of booster events with Dillon's glitterati, someone had to keep everyone fed, clothed, and reasonably on schedule, and Tami was an intimidating master of their shared domain.

Besides, Eric is . . . well, kind of bumbling when it comes to having any idea of what the heck he's supposed to do at home, anyway. He can't brood and bark his way through Tami—she's quicker on her feet than he is, and she'd bark back, louder and more effectively than he could even dream of. The question is how in God's name he managed to get anything on his agenda done at all. And as a public figure, the fact is, he has to—he needs her as part of his image, and in no small capacity. For him, she needs to be everything from arm candy to the perfect hostess—ironic roles for a woman who, by season three, outranks him at his day job. So what's a guy to do?

In a surprisingly savvy move, Eric takes a tack that wives have been using on their husbands since Eve: lie. Well, maybe don't *lie*, lie—after all, it's damn near impossible to cater a party for the entire town without at least clueing your wife in to the fact that they might be arriving and will likely expect to be served something edible. But saving the announcement of said party until the last possible second, when it's impossible to back out without looking like a bad hostess? Totally doable. Your wife will want to save face, even if she hates you.

In fact, Eric does this sort of thing a lot. Over and over again. Need your wife to show up at a football event at a crappy car dealership? Let someone else tell her, in public. First rivalry week since he's been head coach? Why bother saying anything about the barbecue your family will be hosting for half of Dillon High, plus their parents and the football boosters, at all? After all, it'll get around before you know it. In fact, Julie's friend Lois, "the last person in the entire state of Texas to find out about anything," was the one who ended up breaking that particular bit of news to Tami (*via* Julie) ("Who's Your Daddy?" 1-4). And through it all, Eric rather effectively played the innocent card—after all, it was his first year as head coach, so how was he supposed to know of such traditions?

(I don't know, Eric, the fact that you were assistant coach of the same team for six years prior could have given you an idea of what to expect.)

Yes, it seems that Eric has mastered the art of asking for forgiveness, rather than permission. There are few instances, in fact, where he proactively addresses anything with Tami unless he's forced to by the hands of time, although sometimes it's hard to blame him, particularly when it involves Buddy Garrity, as it so often does. I can think of very few wives who would welcome such a desperate creep into their home, and that's assuming they could get past the striking resemblance to an awkward, bloated version of Sam the Eagle gracing their doorstep. I'm not sure I'd want to tell her that he was coming to Thanksgiving either, especially since he's likely to be lecherously running his hands up the thighs of her other dinner guests without their permission. (And it turns out, he did.)

Eric only *truly* lied once, when he told Tami the $3,000 check he wrote to cover the team's uniforms was for the dry cleaning. Frankly, it was hideous and cringe-worthy, both the circumstances that led to the dishonesty and the ease with which he delivered the falsehood. But considering the stress they were both under (unprecedented work challenges for Eric and having the two of them pitted against each other professionally), I can't help but give Eric a pass there. Getting those uniforms was important for the team, yes, but for Eric, it was a symbol of his fate in East Dillon: a sign that he would live to fight another day. (See how I have your back there, Eric? Call me!)

Takeaway: Take a tip from the women of the world—and, um, Eric Taylor: practice strategic omission and the occasional white lie. Encourage husband to do the same. Everybody wins! Or, at least, everyone spends a lot less time being stressed out.

The Result: A Beautiful Disaster

I'm not sure anyone with a lick of sense gets married with the expectation that it will be easy. But what's so hard is that the real challenges are never what you expect. You can brace for the things you see coming—after all, Tami's ex-boyfriend Mo Mac-Donald was never a real threat, despite Eric's posturing (and, later, punching). It's what seems insignificant that can sneak up on you. Living with another person is hard—almost impossible, even. It's a constant negotiation, from whose career takes precedence to who gets the kids breakfast to who the hell is going to pick up the fifty pounds of barbecue ribs.

Oh, and once you've figured that out, you're supposed to still find this person attractive—have sex, even!—despite the fact that your husband's meeting ran longer than expected, leaving you to ditch work early to pick up the kids. Or that you just can't bring yourself to move past that morning's battle of the dirty boxers on the floor. Or, you know, that your wife just told you that you were fired. Things like that.

For the Taylors, the mix of a petulant teenager, a surprise pregnancy, dueling careers, and the omnipresent (and ever-disgusting) Buddy Garrity and half of Dillon High showing up at all hours of the night means it's a year-round Christmas miracle that no one runs screaming from the building, gets in the car, and makes a run for the border in search of a peaceful existence as a beachcomber.

It's a dance only for the very brave or the very naïve. Probably both. And yet, the Taylors do it beautifully, and demonstrate that with a little perseverance and a lot of patience, you will be richly rewarded with a deeper connection and what most of us got into this mess for in the first place: a true companion and partner who loves you unconditionally, no matter what life brings. And what makes the Taylors so perfect is that they *never* make it look easy.

When the series ends, we are left knowing that no matter what happens, the Taylors will survive. Even after watching Eric make the ultimate sacrifice of his job—and life, really—in Dillon to give Tami the chance to pursue her dream as a college admissions counselor in Philadelphia, we are confident that, somewhere, Eric and Tami are happier than ever.

And if the cost of perfection is a lot of booze and a few white lies, well, I think we'd all gladly pay that price—provided the wine is good enough.

WHY WE LOVE
. . . Coach Eric Taylor

Coach Eric Taylor is a real man.

Yes, he can be called that for a lot of the traditional reasons.

He is fiercely protective of his women, both his wife, Tami, and, especially, his two daughters. He is also occasionally flummoxed by them.

He can be stubborn and unforgiving, especially when he thinks one of his players has acted irresponsibly or that anyone—be it Buddy Garrity or Joe McCoy—is questioning his coaching authority.

And he loves, lives, and breathes his football. We're pretty sure that when Eric Taylor lies down next to Tami each night and closes his eyes, he's orchestrating plays in his dreams.

But all that stereotypical male behavior aside, Eric Taylor also happens to be a man in the very best, most honorable sense of the word. He truly elevates the gender.

He cherishes his marriage and lets Tami know daily how much he loves her.

No matter how stressful family life becomes, Eric usually keeps the problems in perspective and his blessings properly counted. ("That is not our burden," he once told Tami when she started to panic about finding childcare for baby Gracie. "That is our gift.")

And as a coach, he is more than just an athletic mentor. He is, as Tami and even Billy Riggins told him, a molder of men, a dad of two daughters by blood but an infinite number of sons on the football field. And there was truly nothing Coach would not do for his kids.

He made sure Smash Williams secured a spot at Texas A&M. He threw Matt Saracen into a cold shower and screwed his head on straight when his team and his grandmother needed him to be a leader. He turned Vince Howard into an East Dillon Lion and kept him out of jail. He stood before a parole board and with his words—"He is a good young man, and that's how I know him"—helped Tim Riggins get out of jail.

With the mantra that he devised and repeated before every Dillon Panther game, he instilled a set of principles in his soon-to-be-molded men every Friday night. Coach didn't encourage his team to scrap their way to victory or to try to obliterate their opponents—terms like "win" or "beat 'em senseless" are notably absent from the Eric Taylor catchphrase. He simply wanted them to play with as much passion and dignity as their teenage spirits could muster. And if they did that, then they would know they had achieved something, scoreboard be damned.

Or, to put it in Eric's words:

Clear eyes.

Full hearts.

Can't lose.

Throughout the course of *Friday Night Lights*, Eric Taylor dealt with big problems and faced major decisions: about where to coach, when to fight for his job, and how to realize his dreams while also making sure that Tami realized hers. We loved him for the way he handled all of that. Fine, we didn't love him as much when it took him ages to properly celebrate Tami's job offer at Braemore College. But we figured he'd come around, and he did.

That said, what we loved even more about Eric—and, really, about so much of *Friday Night Lights*—were the little moments. The way he pursed his lips just before he went on a tirade. The way he whispered "You're a good man" to Jason Street when the QB lay paralyzed in a hospital bed. The way that he charmingly kissed Tami and asked, "What're you doin' tonight?" and knew that the right response to "Nothing" was "I'll get the wine."

Naturally, it's impossible to mention all the subtleties and small acts that make us love Eric Taylor. But here are a few.

- Not many men can look sexy while wearing a windbreaker, khaki shorts, white socks, and a pair of sneakers. Eric Taylor is one of those men.
- Eric once scared a bashful Matt Saracen off the Taylors' sofa, away from Julie, and out of their house. He had a good reason, though. As he accusingly noted of Matt and Julie: "They had a blanket."
- Coach Taylor was a football guy through and through, but he made sure to support the cheerleaders at a crucial competition. That support had nothing to do with preventing Julie from going to an all-day music festival with Matt Saracen. (Eric: "We're all going. It's the cheerleading divisional championship title." Tami: "No, it is not, it's the Cheerleading Classic." Eric: "Well, I didn't read the whole email but it's important and we're all going.")
- When his friend Buddy Garrity came to Eric to confide in him about "straying outside his marriage," Eric was totally willing to listen: "No, no, I'm saying uh-uh. I don't want to know who it is and I don't want to know anything about it."
- In the history of television and possibly moving pictures in general, no husband has ever reacted to an unexpected

pregnancy with more joyful surprise and genuine love than Eric Taylor did when a nervous Tami told him she was expecting. After viewing the scene roughly twenty times, we still need a tissue to get through it.

- Coach Taylor has many gifts. But perhaps his greatest is his ability to make a hell of a locker room speech. "Every man at some point in his life is going to lose a battle," he told the Panthers during halftime of the state championship game that would eventually see them come back and win. "He's going to fight and he's going to lose. But what makes him a man is that in the midst of that battle, he does not lose himself. This game is not over. This battle is not over." After hearing that, even we were ready to suit up and play.

- Shortly after he permanently returned to Dillon following his stint at TMU, Eric made an extra effort to make Tami's life easier. He bought her tulips. He stayed up with Gracie overnight, then got up early and made breakfast. He even created a chart of weekly Taylor events and insisted that Tami go to her Wednesday-night book-club meeting. "A man takes care of his wife," he announced. A man also buys tulips, makes breakfast, and creates charts when he wants to get laid.

- Eric was not immune to jealousy and sometimes expressed it in adorably awkward fashion. Example: the time he told Tami that he did not appreciate her friendship with Dillon High teacher Glenn Reed, with whom he claimed she was always "yukking it up" in the halls. "It's goofy," he said, his expression deadly serious.

- When Tami developed such a complex about sending Gracie to day care that she contemplated quitting her guidance counselor job, Eric talked her out of it: "If years later, it turns out that day care screwed her up, she's always got you for counseling."

- Eric Taylor is a man of few words. But when he's angry, he chooses them really well. After Joe McCoy said that he would not try to get Eric fired as long as he promised that J.D. would start every game the following season—"Against my better judgment, I am offering you an opportunity to continue with this team"—Eric responded with appropriate curtness: "Well, I'm sure you know what you can do with that opportunity."

- On another occasion, an angry Eric also chose his words with a pointed sense of economy. The occasion? His conversation with Matt Saracen after he discovered the boy in bed with his daughter. "I know your father's in Iraq, but if he was here I think he'd agree on one thing, he and I. The both of us," he said. "And that is: women are to be respected. That is my daughter." Yeah, that about covers it.

- Having learned an important lesson from the brawl with Tami's ex-boyfriend Mo MacArnold, Eric opted not to punch Glenn when he informed Eric that he kissed Tami after a happy hour. Later, though, he did lay a pretty creative guilt trip on Tami. "Do you realize," he asked his wife, "that by proxy I have now kissed Glenn?"

- Even though Eric and Julie weren't always on the same wavelength, he could read her mind when it mattered. Shortly after Matt Saracen's father died, Eric took one look at her grieving face, embraced his daughter, and whispered, "I'm not going anywhere."

- Eric's sensitivity to women didn't end when he stepped outside his estrogen-heavy household. When he accidentally caught his equipment manager, Jess Merriweather, crying in the locker room after her breakup with Vince, he didn't tell her there's no crying in football. Instead he said: "You know I've got two daughters, don't you? You take all the time that you need."

- When Eric sat down to have lunch with Jason Street, more than four years after that awful accident on the Panthers field, they faced each other as fellow fathers. And in classic dad fashion, Eric remembered to bring a gift for his favorite QB's son: a Lions cap that had "a little spit-up on it—Gracie got that on there." Um, it's the thought that counts?

When the *Friday Night Lights* story comes to an end, we see Eric Taylor pretty much where we saw him from the beginning, standing on a football field, barking out orders and molding men.

He is in Philadelphia, a city he chose because one of its universities chose his wife. And wherever Tami goes, Eric will follow.

In the final moments of the series, he called together the members of his new team, the Pemberton Pioneers. They didn't look like the Dillon Panthers yet. Hell, they didn't even appear to be the East Dillon Lions when they were in forfeit mode. But they had potential, because they had Eric Taylor standing in front of them, leading the way.

Coach Taylor gave them a brief pep talk, then tried to conclude with that familiar catchphrase.

"Clear eyes," he said.

Blank looks from the Pemberton Pioneers.

"Full hearts," he added.

More blank looks from the Pemberton Pioneers.

"We'll deal with the rest later," he conceded.

There was Eric Taylor, still coaching, out on the field and under the lights. And a few seconds later, his wife, Tami, was right by his side.

The words "can't lose"? They went without saying.

Compare [*Friday Night Lights'* social complexity] to *The West Wing*'s patronizing strategy for bipartisan ratings: a neoliberal presidential administration appreciates that its left flank is obviously naive (why is this obvious?) but is repeatedly surprised by the human decency of its conservative opposition (why is this surprising?). I love *The West Wing*, but if I had to choose I'd take *Friday Night Lights* every time.

—**Steve Thorngate**, "A show about dependence," ChristianCentury.org

[*Friday Night Lights*] is not a political show, except that it's about those things politicians like to lay claim to: community, values, faith, the little guy, the kids.

—**James Poniewozik**, "Farewell to *FNL*: Bridging America's Divides," Time.com

Come Home: West Texas Identities

JACOB CLIFTON

1. Texas Radio

> "Wait, so in West Texas do they really have a radio show
> about *high school football?*"
> "In West Texas they have entire *stations* about high
> school football."
> "Okay. But what do they talk about the rest of the year?"
> "Um, what . . . What do you mean?"

It was the holiday season of 2006, and my friend Ali's husband, Mike, had recorded the first four or five episodes of *Friday Night Lights* and—like the rest of America—was planning on watching them some day that never quite came. I was visiting them in Dallas, like I do most years, and we'd come across the episodes on the TiVo and, being cozy inside and unwilling to leave the couch—I think there might have been literal ice cream involved—we turned it on.

Alison's an attorney, and I never stop working, so the idea of spending the day in bed with a TV show seemed novel, maybe even a little dangerous. I was uncomfortable with discussing my West Texas provenance, or playing resident expert, two things viewing a show with *Friday Night Lights'* setting normally would have led to. But we'd gone to college together, and I knew she knew my painful secret. We thought it was an experiment in sloth.

But by the time Jason Street was down and Eric Taylor was leading his boys in prayer, it felt like we were doing anything *but* playing hooky from life. We were engaged, leaning forward, screaming at the screen, for the rest of the day. And when Mike came home from work, we started over again from the beginning.

As a TV critic, I've come to learn that the things I love most, the movies and stories that I can honestly say have changed my life, generally turn out to be the ones I can't immediately assess. Most people like the things they like, and dislike the things they don't. I understand that it generally works that way, but it's rare that it does for me. The films of Ang Lee, the more recent show *The Good Wife*: I still can't tell you why I love them, only that I do—and with my whole self.

That cold Dallas day was five years ago, but I think I'm only beginning to understand exactly why *Friday Night Lights* affects me the way that it does. And it's at once as coldly quantifiable, and totally personal, as only the best art can be.

2. About vs. "About"

Try telling somebody who's never seen the show how good it is, and you know what they'll say: it's a show about football. Try telling somebody from West Texas how good it is, and they'll say, "I lived through that the first time."

From 1993–1995, I attended Midland's Robert E. Lee High School (Team: The Lee Rebels), whose Confederate flag only recently came down. Our rival school is Odessa Permian, whose 1988 Panthers lineup was the subject of Bissinger's book. In some ways a sore subject, the book and later movie were discussed in quiet tones that had faded altogether by the time the show came around.

At worst, from simply flipping past or seeing a commercial, the show's visual beauty and complex issues gave West Texans the impression of a gloss on our little sister-towns: a show "about" us that wasn't really about us at all. At best, it was a reminder of something precious that we might have already lost.

Of course, that's if you haven't seen it. If you know the show, you know it's about a much larger "us."

3. Money & No Money

To understand West Texas, the politics and identities that distinguish it from the rest of the world, is first to understand Texas. Neither South nor North, neither Midwest nor Coastal, Texas is its own strange thing. Our collective national images of Texas— big skies, cowboys, guns, and millionaires—are not entirely off-base. Texas combines the frontier pride of the other horse states (Wyoming, Montana) with the peculiarities of its size. Texas is gigantic, and even with its three major urban complexes and their suburbs, there's enough space left over—full of towns, lives, histories—that those cities don't even describe its essence.

And then way up toward the Panhandle, at the top and western end of Texas, bordering New Mexico and Oklahoma, you get the Permian Basin, from which our country still gets one-fifth of its petroleum. The Texas oil business is administrated almost entirely out of Midland and Odessa. Until the Oil Bust in the mid-80s, that meant an economy based almost entirely on the oil industry: lawyers, luxuries, assayers, riggers, insurance companies, and the rest rose and fell based on oil futures and crude prices. Mostly rose. After the Bust, those boutique industries were forced to merge into larger companies or risk fading altogether, and the archetypal Oil Baron became a relic. Those who sold well stayed on top; those who braved it out or sold poorly never quite got back on the horse.

In most small-town stories, you have a pretty wide class array, plenty of economic strata to play with. Most southern writers, McCullers and Percy to Flagg and Faulkner, assemble southern types in just this way; Harper Lee's *To Kill a Mockingbird* is in some ways a strict meditation on the ways negotiating these concerns led to the creation of whole identities.

What sets an Odessa or Midland story apart—and thus sets apart the characters in play—is the near absence of a middle class. On a national scale, the per-capita earnings of a single upper-class household may not seem like much to those outside the region, but in the tiny oil-bubble economy of West Texas, money has its own meaning and its own scale. (One of the few southern aspects of Texas, in fact, is the agreed-upon disconnect between *money* and *class*.)

On the first three seasons of the show, for example, the only time money came up—beyond Buddy's constant search for booster contributions, of course—was when J.D. McCoy's family arrived. In the later seasons, of course, you had East Dillon and all the race-class-money complications that arise there, but the original cast had very little to say about money. That wasn't a mistake or oversight, and wasn't a result of other story priorities: it's that this kind of conflict is a rare thing in West Texas. Between the two monolithic economic levels—*money* and *no money*—there aren't a lot of shades of gray. If there were interactions between the two, there would be explosive conflict, and on occasion, of course, there is. But interaction is rare. It's a matter less of antipathy than of geography: in Texas, you have space enough to keep your own self-segregated company.

And even in the post-Bust days (when most of our characters were born), those economic levels didn't really change: the rich got richer and the poor stayed poor, because the Bust had already sorted us all out. We've now entered another Boom: there are estimates currently that around 2,000 jobs are available in the oil fields, with nobody to fill them. But we've all already found our own ways to survive, whether in poverty or otherwise, and the days of hardworking oil-field roughnecks are tip-of-the-tongue history, not a growth industry. It's a bit late in the day for a real oil resurgence, environmentally speaking, and the high-risk nature of the industry isn't as exciting as it was before the Bust.

Taking money out of the equation, dealing with the specifically political and polarizing subject matter of a show like this—race, sexuality, gender roles, the place of religion in public life—may seem like a strange move to make, since we're so used to imputing money when we discuss these things on a national scale. But it's essential to understanding the politics of the show itself.

4. Puppets & Umbrellas

"Conservative" and "liberal" mean different things for a Texan—especially a West Texan—than to the rest of the world. And rather than giving a dry summation of why that is, I can point you to the show itself. Because while the rest of us were labeling states red and blue and blaming each other for everything that ever went wrong, *Friday Night Lights* was softly explaining the culture war in terms that showed the positive on both sides of that conflict, without ever sacrificing the importance of either.

And it's my belief that this show could only ever have taken place in West Texas because of its strange mix of conservatism and liberalism. Neither red nor blue, nor really purple, West Texas takes the strangest aspects of both and slaps them together. As a financial center, you have a Republican majority complaining about taxes, of course, but also investing with pride in our children's education, which is not at all a statewide priority. As the standard bearer for the Wild West, you have lots of guns—but few Second Amendment debates, because we mainly use rifles, and for their intended purpose. You have socially conservative values-voters who are honestly horrified by the bullying and violence that are a direct result of their family- and value-centered causes. And so on.

Because our media has focused so much on itself, on the way it tells its stories and pressures us politically, it can often seem like the other side is only sheep: here Glenn Beck weeping over his gold, there Jon Stewart, smirking his way through another yokel interview, everybody doing what they're told. Because we're only talking to ourselves, those stark political lines can start to seem like the reality. And even if you get close enough to "them" to investigate further, you might still come away convinced you were right all along.

Republicans *do* vote with their hearts, not their heads. Glenn Beck *is* a puppetmaster. Or, alternately, Democrats *do* live entirely within their own superiority. Jon Stewart *is* a pundit hiding under his I'm-no-pundit umbrella.

5. Fight Songs

But look a little closer yet, through the lens of Peter Berg, and things start to look a little different. Maybe it's because of the lush documentary filming style, with its balletic choreography of handheld cameras. Maybe it's the improvised-feeling, naturalistic acting of the show's talented cast. Heck, maybe it's the Greek chorus of the football radio.

Or maybe it's because all of these things, through their artifice, manage to show you things more clearly than you might have been able to perceive on your own. Which is the role of all great art, isn't it?

Because what the show can show you is that liberals don't just live in their own superiority: they believe in the potential for *everybody's* superiority, because that's really just another definition for *equality*. Tami Taylor couldn't get up in the morning without that thought in her head, and she always couches her feminism (a label she would never claim!) as self-respect: simple and obvious and necessary, not political—certainly not liberal—but essential.

Eric believes with so much of himself in the potential of his boys that when they go wrong he carries that failure on his back and cries himself to sleep, without once thinking of the color of their skin or in which part of town they live. Again: a response neither political nor liberal, but merely a rational and compassionate extension of the relationships he's built with these kids.

And that's the genius of the show: conservatives don't just *vote* with their hearts, they do *everything* with their hearts. Including all those heartless acts that horrify liberals, like trying to ensure their families succeed, and their money doesn't vanish, and that their kids will be competitive enough to survive in the ugly, real world (you know, the one liberals sometimes have trouble admitting exists?). Those slogans—"Clear Eyes, Full Hearts," and pledges of loyalty—"Texas Forever"—actually *mean* something.

They mean touching something larger than yourself and knowing that you are a part of it. That you are loved, in a transpersonal and symbolic way that is simultaneously totally anonymous and completely, forever, yours alone to cherish.

And that is something, a fleeting feeling, that we all know and can remember. If you're anything like me, you're much more likely to well up in the presence of something beautiful than something sad. You get the lump in the throat when you are feeling good, not so much when you're feeling bad. Imagine having that feeling all the time, in response to certain triggers—hearth and home, national defense, the flag and concept of our country themselves, American authenticity in any of its kitschier forms—and you'll understand more about the voting process in this country than a million talking heads could chart for you.

There is no conservative lock on patriotism, any more than liberals have a monopoly on charity. But liberal patriotism looks suspiciously like nitpicking, the attempt to create a better country through constant complaint, and conservative charity looks suspiciously like church.

The only reason flag-burning is a wedge every ten years, the only reason Glenn Beck gets away with the silly, pandering performances he pulls out regularly, is because we differ about *which* symbols and ideas are important. This is patently ridiculous, because the ideals actually *are* the same—or at least the ones that matter, from the pride and complexity of a national identity to the love and hope we have for our children—which is why *Friday Night Lights* rules: it takes away everything dressing up the ideal and then clothes that ideal anew, in compelling characters and dramatic arcs with no political agenda at all.

Or at least not one you would recognize, these days.

6. One Thing & the Other

Name a purely conservative character on *Friday Night Lights*. No? How about a purely liberal character, there's got to be at least one silly or glib . . . no? Not even that awful little lesbian?

Well, how about the minorities, they can't be voting Republican. Oh, they're generally portrayed as more religiously (and sometimes socially) conservative than anybody else? What about that one annoying girlfriend of Smash's? She was a vegetarian or something . . . Nope: pastor father and the stigma of mental illness.

And this complexity isn't a case of Hollywood character-creation, either. They're all real West Texas archetypes *and* real people, which unlike your political foes are never solely one thing or the other. (I knew at least one Jason Street, and about twenty Tim Rigginses, and those boys loved each other even more, if it's possible, than do their TV counterparts.)

The whole time it aired, the favorite show among U.S. senators, without regard to political affiliation, was overwhelmingly *The West Wing*. Perhaps this was narcissism—definitely, a little bit, it was—but it was also because the show was unfailingly compassionate toward every viewpoint, respectful to the humanity of every complaint, damning of lazy partisanship from every direction, and all in a way that was as moving as it was rare.

Friday Night Lights, in its embattled way, took up that mantle. The show is pretty direct, though I wouldn't say "unflinching," about the sometimes ugly, behind-the-scenes parts of conservatism: gender biases, issues of race and religion, the profit motive, the usual demons of the Right.

But what the show is also doing, and so well and so palatably you might miss it completely, is showing the positive aspects of that same order of philosophy—team play, leadership, military service, patriotism, even religious work—in a way that doesn't ping liberal sensibilities.

You might not even know you were learning about conservative values at all: to see the show tell it, you might just think you were looking at the finest things of which human beings are capable.

7. War Movies

The concept of the football team—as something you would die for, get in a bar fight about, cry in front of your children over even stone-cold sober—is something that makes visceral sense to the conservative mind, and very little sense to anybody else.

Even high school teams: they are still *teams*. The finest move the show makes is helping you to understand *why*. To feel that grip around your heart and lungs you remember getting from the *West Wing* theme song: we are all here, together, doing something remarkable. Simply by living in this country, at this time, you are a member of a team so large and varied it's barely comprehensible.

The show makes you understand that while these boys are compelling individuals on their own, with problems and victories only we get to see, they are also a family of unbelievable rigor, and loyalty, and above all transience. High school football is a war movie that lasts three years at best, but also never really ends.

And you see these themes, of synthesis and compassion beyond the extraneous markers we generally use to describe ourselves, play out everywhere, not muddled together or meeting in the middle but brightly represented, both sides at once.

In the Taylors' robust marriage, with its absolutely equal give-and-take and endless supply of humor, you see what a conservative head of household can be, and often is. In Julie Taylor's religious questioning and Tami's compassion, Landry Clarke's complete lack of judgment or hypocrisy or scorn, you see what a Christian is supposed to be, and often is. In Matt Saracen, you see that even a broken father can pass on the strength of a soldier to his son.

8. All of the Us

By never begging the question or presenting straw-man arguments, as a lot of our entertainment does, *Friday Night Lights* is never drawn down the road of seeing these people as anything but people. And speaking as a gay, liberal atheist from Austin, I'm not making the case for conservatism, or in fact doing anything other than your best and hardest work fighting for your ideals, whatever they are. I'm only making the case—as the show does—for humans, for your fellow Americans. For your people. All of the us.

And I don't think without this show I would be able to say that with any kind of conviction at all, because the noise has gotten so loud and everybody's using the same tricks, regardless of where they sit along the political aisle. I don't think that I would have been able to go home, or even to think of it *as* home, without that show giving me clearer eyes and a fuller heart than I ever would have believed possible.

Because now, when I think of West Texas, it's with Eric Taylor in mind, under a blazing sky. It's all those boys dropping to their knees, in silence, the day Six fell. It's knowing that Tami would never, ever choose a life other than the one she's got. It's in knowing that I don't have to be wheelchair-bound to someday become half as good a man as Jason Street.

It's in knowing that what I thought was impenetrable, impossible, too complex to ever really explain—how something as unique as I always found myself came from something so small and tawdry and cheap and close-minded—is not really a problem in any way.

Because I'm not all that special, certainly not all that different from anybody else from Midland or anywhere else. And because that place is not all that small, or tawdry, or cheap, or hateful.

And because I know that no matter where you are from, you don't have any reason to be ashamed. And thanks to *Friday Night Lights*, I don't have to explain any of that when I tell you where I'm from: you already know. And you know, too, that it feels like home.

And you know, every single West Texas expatriate of my acquaintance has eventually said to me, once we were old enough to understand it, or even think it: *Even though I ran screaming from that place the second I could—convinced, as all adolescents are, of my oppression and subjugation and persecution, despite all evidence to the contrary—it's okay to love it, too.*

Maybe even essential.

There's no real sense in eulogizing a five-season run that still felt five seasons too short. It's done been gone. The sets are long since struck in Austin and elsewhere, the cast and crew on to other shows. But [*Friday Night Lights*] was (oh, the "was" hurts) one of those stories that you could pick up midway through, with no introduction, and immediately just get what it was about, with every shot telling a story, or savor every minute of every hour …

It says something about us that even when it's crammed full of decidedly not-real football loaded with questionable calls (don't analyze the gameplay, you'll go mad), we cannot turn away. It says something far, far sadder about the American zeit-geist that the show never got better legs. It's a hollow melancholy that would fit right in in Dillon, Texas. But here again: Don't be sad. It's already over, and its light is just now reaching us, like the last rays of a dead star. That it existed this long at all is a miracle.

—**Holly Anderson**, "Friday Night Lights Series Finale Ends Five-Year Run; Please Remove Your Hats," SBNation.com

Our final scene, appropriately, is of Coach addressing his new players, being tough ("We have a long way to go, gentlemen") yet hopeful ("And you know what? I'm looking forward to it"), eager for the challenge of again building something—not just building a team, but building character. His new kids don't know the "Clear eyes" chant yet, but they will. Coach Eric Taylor will teach them that—and a whole lot more.

—**Alan Sepinwall**, "Series finale review: 'Friday Night Lights'— 'Always': Texas Forever?", What's Alan Watching on HitFix.com

Author Biographies

WILL LEITCH is a contributing editor at *New York* magazine, a film critic at Yahoo, and the founder of Deadspin. He is also the author of four books, most recently *Are We Winning?* He lives with his wife in Brooklyn and owns many attractive hats.

JEN CHANEY is a reporter and blogger for the *Washington Post*, where she covers entertainment and pop culture. She has covered events like the Academy Awards and Comic-Con, and interviewed celebrities ranging from George Clooney to (Tami Taylor alert!) Connie Britton. But the most fulfilling experience of her journalism career thus far involved her obsessive coverage of *Lost*, which—just as this book did—allowed her to justify spending hours in front of the television watching one of her favorite shows.

JACOB CLIFTON is a writer in Austin, Texas. His critical and analytical work writing about television and film can be found at www.TelevisionWithoutPity.com and www.jacobclifton.com. He graduated from Robert E. Lee High School in Midland, Texas, a full three years before the Confederate flag outside came down, the recipient of zero sports scholarships, a fair amount of notoriety, and a chronic inability to understand even the most basic things about football.

JEREMY CLYMAN, MA, is pursuing his doctorate in clinical psychology at Yeshiva University in New York City. In 2007, he graduated from Northeastern University with an MA in journalism with a specialization in mental health. He has written for numerous publications that examine issues of cinema/television and mental health and is proud to join the esteemed group of writers at BenBella Books.

KIARA KOENIG is a poet, scholar, and lifelong member of the world's largest dysfunctional family, Raider Nation. She holds an MFA in creative writing, an MA in English literature, and is a professor of English at both Butte College and Shasta College. She currently serves as faculty advisor for *The Haberdasher* literary journal and as Assistant Coach of Individual Events for Butte College's Speech and Debate Team. Though she admits that serving aces isn't quite as satisfying as tackling ball carriers, these days she lets her competitive side out on the tennis court rather than the football field.

PAUL LEVINSON, PhD, is Professor of Communication & Media Studies at Fordham University in NYC. His nonfiction books, including *The Soft Edge* (1997), *Digital McLuhan* (1999), *Realspace* (2003), *Cellphone* (2004), and *New New Media* (2009), have been translated into ten languages. His science fiction novels include *The Silk Code* (1999), *Borrowed Tides* (2001), *The Consciousness Plague* (2002), *The Pixel Eye* (2003), and *The Plot To Save Socrates* (2006). He appears on *The O'Reilly Factor* and numerous TV and radio programs. His 1972 LP, *Twice Upon a Rhyme*, was reissued in 2010. He reviews television in his InfiniteRegress.tv blog, and was listed in *The Chronicle of Higher Education*'s Top 10 Academic Twitterers in 2009.

ARIELLA PAPA has never played team sports, but she would be willing to try if Tim Riggins were the captain. She lives with her family in Brooklyn, New York, and would love to visit Texas someday. She is a television promo writer and producer. She is also the author of *On The Verge, Bundle of Joy?*, and *Up & Out.* Her latest novel, *Momfriends,* is available through her website, www.ariellapapa.com.

PAULA ROGERS is a writer and illustrator based in San Francisco. Her work in print and radio has been featured by San Francisco's KQED Public Radio, National Public Radio, the Third Coast International Audio Festival, and *Salon.* She worked as a copywriter and editor for *Show Me How*, an info-graphic guide to life published by HarperCollins, and currently illustrates new titles in the series. When not deepening her relationship with her computer, she enjoys painting, opining, and nurturing an unhealthy interest in numerous fictional characters.

JONNA RUBIN finds that she's a better wife when Tami and Eric Taylor are on the air, leaving her husband to wonder how much he's really going to enjoy life in a post-*Friday Night Lights* era. Beyond reading and watching copious amounts of television, she spends her days writing, child-wrangling, and drinking many bottles of wine in an effort to find the one that will miraculously turn her into Tami Taylor. A former newspaper editor and journalist, she's also contributed to two other Smart Pop titles, *A Taste of True Blood* and *Filled With Glee.* When not transforming her wardrobe into that of the perfect Texas housewife, she ekes out a living as a freelance writer and blogs about motherhood, pop culture, and life in New England at www.jonniker.com.

SARAH MARIAN SELTZER is an associate editor at AlterNet and freelance writer based in New York City. Her writing on female sexuality and pop culture has been published in the *Washington Post, Publishers Weekly*, and the *Los Angeles Times* and on the websites of *The Nation, The Christian Science Monitor, The Wall Street Journal*, and Jezebel.com. Read more of her writing at www.sarahmseltzer.com.

KEVIN SMOKLER is the author of *Bookmark Now: Writing in Unreaderly Times*, a *San Francsico Chronicle* Notable Book of 2005. His writing has appeared in the *Los Angeles Times, Fast Company, The Believer*, and NPR. He lives in San Francisco.

TRAVIS STEWART is the managing editor of *Dave Campbell's Texas Football* magazine, a biannual publication that covers all levels of football in the state of Texas, with a special emphasis on high schools. *DCTF* magazines appear frequently throughout *Friday Night Lights*—Smash's dashing action shot on one fictitious *DCTF* cover rankled Saracen in season two, for example, as did the dramatic posed shot of J.D. McCoy in the fictional "freshman preview." Travis has worked for *DCTF* since 2007 and is proud to be a part of the Texas high school football community—truly one of the most passionate and endearing fan bases in the world.

ROBIN WASSERMAN has never met a gym class she didn't hate. The prospect of playing a team sport makes her want to crawl under a desk and stay there (an impulse her prospective teammates would surely appreciate once they saw her throwing/kicking/catching skills, or lack thereof). She takes her revenge on the ghosts of gym teachers past by writing them into her young adult novels, which include *Hacking Harvard, Skinned, Crashed, Wired*, and the Seven Deadly Sins series. She admits that if the NFL signed

Tim Riggins and played some stirring music over their games, she might actually be willing to watch the Super Bowl.

ADAM WILSON's first novel, *Flatscreen*, will be published by Harper Perennial in winter 2012. He is the editor of the international newspaper *The Faster Times*, and a former culture columnist for *Blackbook*. His journalism, criticism, and fiction have appeared in many publications including *Bookforum*, the *New York Times*, the *New York Observer*, the *Paris Review Daily*, *Meridian*, *Washington Square Review*, *Gigantic*, *Time Out New York*, *The Forward*, *Paste*, *Boldtype*, *The Rumpus*, and the anthologies *Dirty Words: A Literary Encyclopedia of Sex* and *Promised Lands: New Jewish Fiction on Longing and Belonging*. He lives in Brooklyn with his cat.

LEAH WILSON is Editor-in-Chief of the Smart Pop imprint of BenBella Books. She lives in Cambridge, Massachusetts.